Introduction to Natural Language Processing
Exploring Techniques, Applications, and Challenges

Published 2025 by River Publishers

River Publishers

Broagervej 10, 9260 Gistrup, Denmark

www.riverpublishers.com

Distributed exclusively by Routledge

605 Third Avenue, New York, NY 10017, USA

4 Park Square, Milton Park, Abingdon, Oxon OX14 4RN

Introduction to Natural Language Processing / by Xiaochun Cheng, Preethi Nanjundan, Jossy P George.

Routledge is an imprint of the Taylor & Francis Group, an informa business

ISBN 978-87-7004-829-3 (paperback)

ISBN 978-87-7004-831-6 (online)

ISBN 978-87-7004-830-9 (ebook master)

A Publication in the River Publishers Rapids Series in *Computing and Information Science and Technology*

While every effort is made to provide dependable information, the publisher, authors, and editors cannot be held responsible for any errors or omissions.

Introduction to Natural Language Processing
Exploring Techniques, Applications, and Challenges

Editors

Xiaochun Cheng

Swansea University, Bay Campus, Wales, UK

Preethi Nanjundan

CHRIST University, Pune Lavasa Campus, India

Jossy P George

CHRIST University, Delhi NCR, India

River Publishers

Routledge
Taylor & Francis Group
NEW YORK AND LONDON

Contents

Abstract

Natural language processing (NLP) is one of the most prominent branches of artificial intelligence (AI), equipped with certain capabilities to enable effective and coherent human–machine communication. The target of this approach consists of processing a vast number of pieces of text/speech in order to extract meaningful information, infer the intention as well as generate appropriate responses. Bridging these interplays between human communication and machine understanding, NLP has opened up a better outlook on the interactions with technology within multiple domains. Key tasks in NLP involve text preprocessing – the cleaning of text and preparing it for analysis through processes like tokenization and removing any extraneous elements, such as stop words. Part-of-speech tagging assigns required grammatical tags to words, while named entity recognition detects the most relevant entities, such as people, organizations, and dates. Another significant task is sentiment analysis, which allows categorization of the emotional state described through the text, whether it is positive, negative, or neutral. Language modeling amounts to predicting the sequence of words through context; a pretty neat trick with a practical application in machine translation, in which input from one linguistic space is outputted into another. Question answering enables extraction of pertinent answers from vast datasets. Applications of the NLP techniques are wide-ranging, from customer service to healthcare and fraud detection; really, any field from where data is extracted. Recently, new developments such as deep learning models, enlarged annotated databases, and current powerful computational possibilities have raised and transformed NLP into much wider applications in machine translation, language understanding, and answer generation. Its increasing impact shows NLP is continuing to play a vital role in further advancing human–computer interactions across all sectors.

Preface

The most valuable acquisitions in a scientific or technical education are the general-purpose mental tools which remain serviceable for a lifetime.

— George Forsythe, "What to do till the computer scientist comes." (1968)

Natural language processing (NLP) is a subfield of artificial intelligence (AI) that focuses on the interaction between computers and human language. It involves the development of algorithms and techniques that enable machines to understand, interpret, and generate natural language, such as text or speech.

NLP aims to bridge the gap between human communication and machine understanding. By analyzing and processing vast amounts of textual data, NLP systems can extract meaningful information, infer intent, and generate appropriate responses. This technology has numerous applications, ranging from language translation and sentiment analysis to chatbots and voice assistants.

At its core, NLP involves several key tasks:

1. **Text preprocessing:** Before analyzing text, it often needs to be preprocessed. This step includes tokenization (splitting text into individual words or sentences), removing punctuation, converting text to lowercase, and handling stop words (commonly used words like "the" or "and" that may not carry much meaning).
2. **Part-of-speech tagging:** This process involves assigning grammatical tags (such as noun, verb, adjective, etc.) to each word in a sentence, providing information about its role and function within the sentence.
3. **Named entity recognition (NER):** NER involves identifying and classifying named entities, such as names of people, organizations, locations, dates, or numerical values, in a given text.
4. **Sentiment analysis:** This task includes defining the sentiment articulated in a text, whether it is positive, negative, or neutral. It can be used for customer feedback analysis, social media monitoring, or brand reputation management.

5. **Language modeling:** Language models are designed to predict the likelihood of a sequence of words in a given context. They are trained on vast amounts of textual data and can generate coherent and contextually appropriate text.
6. **Machine translation:** NLP techniques are also used in machine translation systems, which automatically translate text from one language to another. These systems employ various approaches, such as statistical methods, rule-based systems, or neural machine translation.
7. **Question answering:** NLP enables systems to understand and respond to user questions by extracting relevant information from a given text corpus or knowledge base.

Over the years, NLP has made significant advancements, driven by the availability of large annotated datasets, the development of deep learning models, and the increased computational power. These advancements have led to substantial improvements in tasks such as machine translation, sentiment analysis, and language understanding.

NLP has a wide range of practical applications across industries, including customer support, healthcare, finance, e-commerce, and more. As the field continues to evolve, researchers and developers are exploring new techniques and models to further enhance language understanding and generation capabilities, making NLP an exciting and rapidly growing area of research and development.

About the Editors

Dr. Xiaochun Cheng is at Swansea University, Wales, UK, specializing in artificial intelligence, data science, and natural language processing (NLP). With extensive experience in computational linguistics, Dr. Cheng has published numerous papers in top-tier journals and actively contributes to advancing AI research.

Dr. Preethi Nanjundan is an Associate Professor and Research head at CHRIST University, Pune Lavasa Campus, India, with 20 years of experience in research and teaching. Her expertise spans machine learning, neural networks, and NLP, and she has published over 40 papers and several books. She is also a lifetime member of professional bodies like IEEE and CSI.

Dr. Jossy P George is a distinguished professor in the Department of Data Science and the Dean and Director at CHRIST University, Delhi NCR Campus, India. His research interests include data analytics, machine learning, and NLP, with significant contributions to both academia and industry. He plays a pivotal role in mentoring students and leading collaborative research projects.

List of Abbreviations

AI	Artificial Intelligence
NLP	Natural language processing
NER	Named entity recognition
POS	Part-of-speech
TF-IDF	Term frequency-inverse document frequency
ML	Machine learning
RNN	Recurrent neural network
LSTM	Long short-term memory
HMM	Hidden Markov model
SVM	Support vector machine
API	Application programming interface
SLU	Spoken language understanding
BERT	Bidirectional encoder representations from transformers
GPT	Generative pre-trained transformer
CNN	Convolutional neural network.

CHAPTER

1

Introduction

1.1 Introduction to Natural Language Processing (NLP)

The field of computational linguistics and artificial intelligence known as "nat-ural language processing" (NLP) focuses on the interactions between computers and human language. It involves developing and putting into use algorithms and models to understand, decode, and generate human language in a way that is useful and meaningful for humans.

Making it possible for computers to read, understand, and produce natural language text or voice is the aim of NLP. By processing and comprehending human language, NLP enables machines to do tasks like language translation, sentiment analysis, information extraction, question answering, text summa-rization, speech recognition, and more [1].

NLP techniques utilize a combination of linguistics, statistical models, machine learning, and deep learning methods. The method typically involves several steps, including:

Text preprocessing: This step involves cleaning and transforming raw text data, including tasks such as tokenization (breaking text into words or sentences), removing punctuation and stop words, and normalizing text (e.g., converting all characters to lowercase).

Morphological analysis: In this step, the structure and meaning of individual words are analyzed, taking into account features like inflection, tense, and stemming (reducing words to their base or root form).

Syntax and parsing: The grammatical organization of sentences is looked at in this step, and the relationships between words are formed. Part-of-speech tagging, parsing, and syntactic analysis are just a few of the techniques used to understand sentence syntax and structure.

Semantics and meaning: NLP aims to understand the meaning of text beyond its grammatical structure. Methods like named entity identification, semantic role labeling, and word sense disambiguation are used to infer the meaning of words and phrases in context.

Machine learning and deep learning: NLP heavily depend on statistical and machine learning methods to build models that can be trained on a massive quantity of labeled information. These models can be used in many different tasks, including sentiment analysis, text classification, machine translation, and, more recently, the application of deep learning models such as transformers and recurrent neural networks (RNNs).

Natural language generation: NLP is not only about understanding text but also about generating human-like text. Natural language generation (NLG) techniques are used to mechanically produce text that is coherent, informative, and contextually relevant [2].

Applications of NLP are diverse and can be found across many different fields, such as chatbots and virtual assistants for customer service (like Siri and Alexa), language translation services, social media analysis, information retrieval systems, and healthcare applications, to name just a few.

NLP is an active and rapidly evolving field with ongoing research and development. Researchers and practitioners are continually exploring new techniques and models to improve the accuracy and capabilities of NLP systems, making it an exciting area at the connection of language, artificial intelligence, and data science.

1.2 Background and Overview History

The study of natural language processing began after World War II. People at the time recognized the importance of language translation and worked to create a system that could carry out this kind of translation automatically. The task was much more difficult than people had previously believed. In 1958, some academics started highlighting significant issues with the development of NLP.

One of these researchers, Noam Chomsky, was troubled by the way in which language models regarded nonsense sentences that adhered to grammar rules as irrelevant in the same way as nonsense sentences that did not. The fact that the statements "Colorless green ideas sleep furiously" and "Furiously sleep ideas green colorless" were regarded as equally unlikely worried Chomsky. Chomsky believed that human standards should apply to machine models as well, but that this was not the case.

Between 1957 and 1970, researchers divided into two distinct groups to study NLP: symbolic and stochastic. Many linguists and computer scientists focused on formal languages and developing syntax in symbolic, or rule-based, research, which they considered as the beginning of artificial intelligence research. Those who studied optical character recognition and textual pattern recognition were increasingly interested in statistical and probabilistic approaches to NLP.

Computers can understand, interpret, and utilize human languages thanks to a feature of artificial intelligence called natural language processing (NLP). Machines can communicate with people using human language thanks to NLP. Natural language processing allows computers to read text, hear speech, and understand it. NLP utilizes a range of disciplines, such as computational linguistics and computer science, to close the communication gap between humans and computers.

In general, NLP breaks down language into smaller, more fundamental pieces known as tokens in order to understand the relationships between the tokens (words, periods, etc.). This process commonly employs higher-level NLP components, such as:

- Content categorization: Content categorization is a linguistic document summary that includes content alerts, duplicate identification, search, and indexing.
- Topic discovery and modeling: With the use of sophisticated analytics, this technique uncovers the main ideas and concepts in text collections.
- Contextual extraction: automatically extracts structured data from text-based sources.
- Sentiment analysis: This technique identifies the overall feelings or viewpoints buried in massive amounts of text; it is useful for gaining perspectives.
- Text-to-speech and speech-to-text conversion: Using these technologies, written instructions can be converted into spoken ones.
- Document summarization: Automatically creates a summary from large amounts of material.
- Machine translation: Automatically translates spoken or written words from one language into another.

1.3 Applications of NLP

Natural language processing (NLP) has numerous uses across a wide range of industries and fields. Here are about some common applications of NLP:

Sentiment analysis: NLP techniques are used to determine the sentiment or opinion stated in a piece of text, such as social media posts, customer reviews, or survey responses. It is used by businesses to analyze customer feedback, monitor brand reputation, and make data-driven decisions.

Language translation: Natural language processing (NLP) is a key component of machine translation systems, which automatically translate text or speech from one language to another. Systems like Google Translate use NLP algorithms to decipher sentence meaning and deliver accurate translations.

Information extraction: Structured data can be extracted from unstructured text using NLP algorithms. Named entity recognition (NER) is a method for locating and categorizing named entities, such as specific individuals, teams, locations, and dates. Relation extraction identifies relationships between entities, and event extraction captures specific events mentioned in the text.

Question answering: NLP-based question answering systems interpret questions posed in natural language and provide relevant answers. These developments make it possible for chatbots, virtual helpers, and search engines to answer to user inquiries with speed and accuracy.

Text summarization: NLP is used to automatically generate summaries of large documents or articles. This makes it much simpler to create succinct summaries of extensive reports and document summaries for research requirements.

Chatbots and virtual assistants: NLP controls chatbots and virtual assistants, enabling them towards understand and respond to user queries and provide interactive conversational experiences. These applications are widely used in customer support, e-commerce, and various online services.

Speech recognition: NLP techniques are applied in speech recognition systems to change spoken language into written text. This technology is used in voice assistants, transcription services, voice-controlled devices, and dictation software.

Text classification: NLP permits the automatic classification of text documents into predefined categories. It consumes applications in spam detection, sentiment analysis, news categorization, content filtering, then fraud detection.

Information retrieval: NLP techniques enhance the effectiveness of information retrieval systems by understanding user queries and matching them to relevant documents. Search engines use NLP algorithms to provide accurate search results and improve the user search experience.

Healthcare applications: NLP is used in healthcare to analyze medical records, extract relevant information, and improve clinical decision-making. It aids in tasks such as information extraction from medical literature, patient diagnosis, disease classification, and adverse event detection [3].

These are just a few examples of the numerous applications of NLP. As the field continues to advance, new applications and use cases are constantly emerging, making NLP a highly dynamic and impactful area of research and development.

The intricacy of our own languages is rarely taken into account. To convey knowledge and meaning, this intuitive activity makes use of semantic cues like words, signs, or images. Language is said to be easier to learn and to come more effortlessly during adolescence since it is a repetitive, learnt behavior, comparable to walking. The fact that there are so many exceptions, such as "I before E except after C," shows that language doesn't strictly follow a set of rules. What comes naturally to individuals is tremendously difficult for computers since there is so much unstructured data, no explicit rules, and no real-world context or intent. As a result, artificial intelligence (AI) and machine learning are becoming more and more popular. This is because people are increasingly depending on computing systems for communication and task completion. Natural language processing (NLP) will also advance in sophistication along with AI and augmented analytics. Although the phrases artificial intelligence (AI) and natural language processing (NLP) can conjure up ideas of futuristic robots, NLP is already being used in some simple ways in our everyday lives. Here are a few well-known instances.

Email filters: Email filtering is one of the first and most basic online applications of NLP. The first to recognize specific words or phrases that signify a spam message are spam filters. But filtering has advanced, much like early NLP adaptations. NLP is one of the more prevalent and current examples of email classification in Gmail. The system classifies emails into primary, social, or promotional categories based on their content. This keeps your inbox, for all

Gmail users, manageable and filled with urgent, important emails you need to review right away and respond to.

Smart assistants: Intelligent assistants like Apple's Siri and Amazon's Alexa can recognize speech patterns, infer meaning, and provide helpful responses thanks to voice recognition. We have come to believe that when we ask Siri a question by saying, "Hey Siri," she understands what we have said and responds appropriately based on the circumstance. We're also getting used to seeing Siri and Alexa appear in our homes and daily lives when we use appliances like the thermostat, light switches, automobiles, and more. Now that assistants like Alexa and Siri have made our lives easier and some chores, like ordering things, simpler, we expect them to understand contextual cues and even like it when they respond humorously or answer questions about themselves. Our interactions will get more personal as these helpers get to know us better. In a New York Times article titled "Why We May Soon Be Living in Alexa's World," it is said that "Something Bigger is Afoot. Alexa's best chance of success is to come in at number three among consumer computing platforms for this decade."

Search results: Search engines make use of NLP to surface pertinent results based on similar search patterns or user intent, making it easier for the average individual to get what they need without being a search-term expert. Google, for example, not only anticipates what popular searches might be related to your query as you type, but it also takes the overall picture into account and determines what you are trying to say rather than the specific search terms. A person can use Google to check the status of a flight, get market information by entering a ticker symbol, or launch a calculator by entering a math equation. These are some variations you could encounter while searching since NLP in search links the confusing question to a relevant entity and generates useful results.

Predictive text: Because they are so common, functions like autocorrect, auto-complete, and predictive text are things we take for granted on our smart-phones. Autocomplete and predictive text are similar to search engines in that they anticipate what to say depending on the words you enter, either finishing the word or suggesting one that is appropriate. In addition, autocorrect will occasionally change words to make the overall message clearer. They also take text from you. Predictive text will become more linguistically adapted the more you use it. As a result, in funny experiments, people will post full phrases made entirely of predictive text on their phones. The results are incredibly intimate and enlightening; in fact, they have drawn media attention from a variety of sources.

Language translation: Grammar-wise, your Spanish assignment is a complete mess, which is one of the unmistakable signs that you duplicate. Translation services used to overlook the reality that many languages have complex sentence patterns and cannot be translated simply, but they have come a long way. Thanks to NLP, online translators can translate languages more accurately and produce grammatically correct results. This is really helpful when attempting to communicate with someone who speaks a foreign language. Additionally, when translating from a different language to your native tongue, tools automatically recognize the target language based on text input.

Digital phone calls: When we hear the statement "this call may be recorded for training purposes," we hardly ever pause to think about what that really implies. It turns out that while these recordings might be used for training if a customer is displeased, most of the time they are just stored in the database for an NLP system to learn from in the future. Automated systems direct customer calls to a service representative or to online chatbots, who respond to customer questions with helpful information. This NLP approach has been utilized by numerous companies, including significant telecom providers. Additionally, NLP enables computers to construct language that resembles human speech. This video of Google Assistant scheduling a haircut shows how automated phone calls can schedule appointments for services like an oil change or haircut.

Data analysis: Natural language capabilities are being integrated into data analysis workflows as more BI vendors offer a natural language interface to data visualizations. Smarter visual encodings are one example; based on the semantics of the input, they produce the best visualization for the task at hand. Users now have more opportunities to evaluate their data using natural language statements or question fragments made up of a variety of comprehensible and insightful keywords. Using language to analyze data reduces the barrier to analytics across enterprises and promotes accessibility outside of the normal community of analysts and software engineers.

Text analytics: Text analytics converts unstructured text input into information that can be evaluated using a variety of linguistic, statistical, and machine-learning techniques. An NLP tool will frequently scan through consumer interactions, such as social media comments or reviews, or even brand name mentions, to see what is being said, even though corporations may find sentiment analysis frightening, especially if they have a significant client base. Brands can utilize analysis of these interactions to learn how well a marketing campaign is working or to keep an eye on the most frequently raised customer problems before choosing how to respond or enhance service for a better customer experience. Other applications of NLP for text analysis include extracting keywords and identifying patterns or organization in unstructured text data. NLP is used for a variety of things in the digital world, and as more businesses and sectors adopt it and see its advantages, this list will grow. The management and automation of lesser tasks by NLP will improve our lives before moving on to more complex ones, even though a human touch is essential for more complex communication challenges.

1.4 Challenges of NLP Ambiguity

Ambiguity is one of the primary issues in NLP. When attempting to determine the meaning of a phrase, we consider a number of different elements, such as the context in which it is used, our own viewpoint, and the way a word is usually used in society. In addition to having multiple possible interpretations depending on the context, words can also change over time. Examples of this phenomenon include homographs, which are two words with the same spelling but different etymologies, and polysemy, which is one word with numerous meanings.

1.4.1 Types of ambiguity

It may be challenging to characterize ambiguity from a technical standpoint. However, there are additional types of ambiguity that relate to natural language and, consequently, artificial intelligence (AI) systems.

Lexical ambiguity: When a phrase can signify numerous different things, there is clear ambiguity of this kind. For instance, in English, "back" can be a noun (back stage), an adjective (back door), or an adverb (back away).

Syntactic ambiguity: This kind of ambiguity in sentences can be resolved syntactically in a number of different ways. The sentence "I heard his cell phone ring in my office" is an illustration. "In my office" can be parsed in two different ways, one of which modifies the noun and the other the verb.

Semantic ambiguity: This form of ambiguity typically pertains to the appropriate way to interpret a sentence. For instance, the phrase in the sentence before might be interpreted to suggest that I was in fact at work or that the phone was present.

Metonymy: The most difficult type of ambiguity is metonymy, which deals with phrases whose literal meaning differs from the metaphorical assertion. For example, when we say that Samsung is calling for new management, we don't mean it literally (although you never know with Samsung these days).

Metaphors: In a metaphor or other type of metonymy, a phrase with one literal meaning is used as a comparison to convey a different meaning. We are not referring to Roger Clemens as a painter when we say, for example, "Roger Clemens was painting the corners."

Since they regularly make allusions to difficult-to-contextualize real-life or made-up information, metaphors can be particularly difficult to handle. When viewed conceptually, metaphors are a type of metonymy where the connection between sentences is based on similarity.

1.4.2 How to Handle Ambiguity?

Language is ambiguous, which makes NLP difficult because a single word, phrase, or sentence might signify several things depending on the circumstance. With the use of tools like expert.ai, we can get rid of uncertainty and produce responses that are more exact when it comes to word meaning. The technique of dealing with ambiguity is referred to as disambiguation in AI theory. These strategies are quite challenging to manage with today's AI systems. I will discuss this topic in more detail in a subsequent article. Handling ambiguity in natural language processing (NLP) is a serious challenge because human language is rich and nuanced. Here are a few techniques and approaches used commonly in NLP to handle ambiguity:

1. **Contextual understanding:** Consider the context in which the ambiguous word or phrase appears. The denotation of a word can vary based on its surrounding words and the overall background of the sentence or document. Understanding the context helps in disambiguating the intended meaning.
2. **Part-of-speech tagging:** Part-of-speech tagging assigns a grammatical category (noun, verb, adjective, etc.) to each term in a sentence. By analyzing the part-of-speech tags, ambiguity can be reduced as different meanings of a word often correspond to different parts of speech.
3. **Named entity recognition (NER):** NER identifies and classifies named entities like person names, locations, organizations, and dates. By recognizing and understanding these entities, the ambiguity associated with them can be resolved to some extent.
4. **Word sense disambiguation:** Word sense disambiguation (WSD) is the process of determining a word's suitable meaning in a certain context. It involves assigning the appropriate sense or definition to a word with multiple possible interpretations. Various algorithms and techniques, such as using pre-existing lexical resources like WordNet or utilizing context-based approaches like word co-occurrence statistics, can be employed for WSD.

5. **Coreference resolution:** Coreference resolution deals with identifying and connecting nouns or pronouns phrases that represent the same entity. Resolving coreferences helps in understanding the relationships between different parts of a text, reducing ambiguity in meaning.

6. **Machine learning and statistical models:** Machine learning algorithms, such as super-vised and unsupervised approaches, can be training on extensive datasets to learn forms and disambiguate meanings. Statistical models, like probabilistic graphical models, can also be used to capture the likelihood of different interpretations given the context.

7. **Contextual embeddings:** Contextual embeddings, such as word embeddings generated by models like BERT (bidirectional encoder representations from transformers), capture the contextual meaning of words. These embeddings can help disambiguate words constructed on the overall background in which they appear.

8. **User feedback and iterative improvement:** In some NLP applications, user feedback can be used to resolve ambiguity. For instance, if a chatbot provides an ambiguous response, user feedback can help the system understand the intended meaning and improve its future responses.

It's significant to note that complete disambiguation is not always pos-sible, as language can be inherently ambiguous. However, by utilizing these techniques and combining them appropriately, NLP systems can significantly reduce ambiguity and improve the accuracy of language understanding and processing.

1.5 Algorithms and Models in NLP

There are numerous algorithms and models utilized in natural language pro-cessing (NLP) to tackle various tasks and challenges. Here are some popular NLP algorithms and models:

1. **Bag-of-words (BoW):** BoW signifies text as a collection of word occurrences, disregarding grammar and word order. It creates a vector representation of a document based on word frequency. BoW is often used for text categorization and information retrieval applications.

2. **Term frequency-inverse document frequency (TF-IDF):** TF-IDF is a numerical statistic that reflects the importance of a word in a document collection terms that appear more frequently in one document than they do in the entire collection are given a higher weight. TF-IDF is useful for keyword extraction, document similarity calculations, and text classification.

3. **Hidden Markov models (HMMs):** HMMs are statistical models used to model sequential data, including text. They are commonly employed for tasks like part-of-speech tagging, named entity recognition, and speech recognition. HMMs use probability distributions to capture the underlying states and transitions between them.

4. **Conditional random fields (CRFs):** CRFs are probabilistic models used for applications that require sequence labeling, such as named entity identification and part-of-speech tagging. They consider the dependencies between neighboring labels and make predictions based on the observed features.

5. **Word2Vec:** Word2Vec is a neural network-based model that acquires word embeddings by representing words as dense, continuous vectors. It captures the semantic relationships between words and is commonly used for tasks like word similarity calculations, language modeling, and improving performance in downstream NLP tasks.

6. **Recurrent neural networks (RNNs)**: RNNs are a specific kind of neural network architecture designed specifically for processing sequential data. Because they can keep track of dependencies throughout time, they are commonly used for applications like language modeling, emotion analysis, and machine translation.

7. **Long short-term memory (LSTM):** LSTM is a variant of RNNs that addresses the vanishing gradient problem, enabling better long-term dependency modeling. LSTMs are widely used in tasks requiring sequence processing, including text generation, sentiment analysis, and named entity recognition.

8. **Transformer models:** Transformer models, such as the well-known T5 (text-to-text transfer transformer), GPT (generative pre-trained transformer), and BERT (bidirectional encoder representations from transformers) have totally changed NLP. By utilizing self-attention mechanisms to take in contextual information, they have achieved cutting-edge results on a range of tasks, including language comprehension, machine translation, and text synthesis.

9. **Sequence-to-sequence models:** Sequence-to-sequence models, often based on encoder-decoder architectures, are used for tasks like machine translation and text summarization. They allow for both variable-length input and output sequences.

10. **Transfer learning and pretrained models:** Pretrained models, such as those mentioned above (BERT, GPT, T5), have become instrumental in NLP. Using smaller labeled datasets, these models can be improved on specific tasks after being trained on massive corpora. Transfer learning from pretrained models has significantly boosted performance and reduced the need for large annotated datasets.

These are just a few examples of the algorithms and models used in NLP.

The field of NLP is continuously evolving, and researchers are constantly exploring new algorithms, architectures, and techniques to enhance language understanding and processing capabilities.

Natural language processing mostly solves the following issues:

Machine translation is the first conventional assignment handed to the creators of NLP technology (it is crucial to note that it has not yet been resolved at the necessary level of quality for today).

Grammar and spell checking, owing to the primary task.

Text classification, processing of text semantic descriptors, one of the most popular activities to date.

Named-entity recognition (NER), (used to filter text input and understand general semantics) defining and selecting objects with specified meanings.

Summarization, the generalization of the text to a shortened version (reinterpreting the text's meaning).

Text generation, one of the activities involved in creating AI systems.

Topic modeling, a technique for searching through large text volumes to uncover buried topics.

It's important to remember that while developing chat-bots, which are interactive AI systems, all these functionalities in modern and authentic natural language processing are commonly merged into one. It is a configuration (system) that streamlines the process of fusing software with user preferences.

The most widely used NLP algorithms at the moment are listed below:

Lemmatization and stemming: We can build natural language processing of the tasks using lemmatization and stemming. Numerous extra morphological word variations work well with it.

You can limit the diversity inside a term to a single root by using these strategies. As an illustration, we can combine the words "singer," "singing," "sang," and "sang" to form the word "sing." We can quickly reduce the quantity of data required and create more effective and dependable NLP algorithms by doing this for each and every phrase in a document or text.

Lemmatization and stemming are pre-processing techniques, so, in order to free up database space before moving on with the project, we can choose between the two NLP algorithms according on our needs.

Lemmatization and stemming can be done in a variety of methods, but they all lead to the same end result: a reduced search space for the given problem.

Topic modelling: In the process of categorizing a text collection using natural language processing methods like topic modeling, "abstract subjects" are sought out. The idea is that we are looking for linguistic patterns in a corpus of texts that will help us categorize and organize the texts into "themes."

The term "latent Dirichlet allocation" refers to one of the most well-liked NLP techniques for topic modeling. You must first create a list of topics that your collection of papers can be applied to in order for this method to be effective.

Each text in your dataset is originally given an arbitrary topic assignment. After that, you refine the idea and assign papers to various themes after several times circling the example.

Keyword extraction: Keyword extraction, which is in charge of devising various ways for extracting a significant number of words and phrases from a collection of texts, is one of the most important tasks in natural language processing. Simply said, all that is done is done to aid in the relevant and systematic arrangement, storage, search, and retrieval of content.

There are numerous keyword extraction algorithms available, and each one approaches this type of problem using a unique set of theoretical and foundational methods.

There are numerous varieties of NLP algorithms; some just extract words, while others extract both words and phrases. Both NLP algorithms and algorithms that do the same task can extract keywords from texts based on their overall content.

Here are a few of the most well-known keyword extraction formulas:

TextRank: The operation of this algorithm is based on the same theory as PageRank. Google employs this method to rank the importance of various websites on the internet.

Term frequency: The inverse document frequency (TF-IDF) method seeks to make the importance of a phrase in a document more understandable. Phrase frequency-inverse document frequency is the full name of TF-IDF. It also takes into account the relationships among the texts in the same corpus.

RAKE: RAKE, or rapid automatic keywords extraction, is a type of NLP approach. This is capable of doing so by extracting keywords and key phrases from a single text without taking into account the content of other documents in the same collection.

1.5.1 Knowledge graph change

A topic, a predicate, and an entity make up knowledge graphs, which define a method of using triples to store information.

One technique for extracting knowledge-getting ordered information from unstructured materials is to use awareness graphs.

Knowledge graphs have become more and more popular in recent years, especially when numerous companies (like Google Information Graph) use them for various goods and services.

Building a knowledge graph requires a variety of NLP techniques, potentially each approach covered on this page. Using more of these techniques will likely result in a knowledge graph that is more detailed and effective.

1.5.2 Words cloud

A word cloud, sometimes known as a tag cloud, is a technique for displaying data. The most important words in a text are highlighted in bold, and less important words are either underlined or not shown at all. In a table, words from a text are shown.

We can utilize word clouds to condense our findings before running more NLP algorithms on our dataset.

1.5.3 Named entity recognition

The method of named entity recognition is crucial for exploring the natural language domain. Its duty is to organize individuals in unstructured text into a variety of predefined categories. This includes specific individuals, groups, dates, dollar amounts, and so forth.

There are two stages to the named entity recognition procedure:

Identification of prospective NER algorithm candidates is done through a method called named entity identification (NEI).

The classification of named entity candidates into one of the specified categories is one of these procedures.

1.5.4 Sentiment analysis

Sentiment analysis is the NLP method that is most frequently used. Emotion analysis is highly useful in instances where consumers offer their ideas and suggestions, such as surveys, reviews, and debates on social media.

The simplest scale to create in an emotion analysis is a three-point scale (positive/negative/neutral). In more complex situations, the result can be a statistical score that can be divided into as many categories as necessary.

Both supervised and unsupervised methods can be used for sentiment analysis. The most used controlled model for sentiment analysis is naïve Bayes.

1.5.5 Text summarization

NLP approaches can aid in the summary of voluminous volumes of text, as the term implies. Text summaries are widely utilized in situations like research projects and news headlines.

Text summarization can be done in two ways: extraction and abstraction. By deleting specific text passages, extraction techniques are used to create the rundown. Abstraction approaches produce summaries by generating new text that conveys the essence of the original content.

Several NLP methods, including LexRank, TextRank, and latent semantic analysis, can be used for text summarization. Using LexRank as an example, this approach assesses sentences according to how similar they are. If there are more comparable sentences and those similar sentences are similar to other sentences, the sentence will receive a higher grade.

1.5.6 Bag of words

This paradigm maintains multiplicity while ignoring syntax and even word order, expressing a text as a bag (multiset) of words. The incidence matrix is fundamentally created by the bag of words paradigm. These word frequencies or instances are used as characteristics in the training of a classifier.

Unfortunately, there are certain problems with this paradigm. The worst part is that these terms are wrongly weighted and lack context and semantic meaning (in this approach, "universe" is given less weight than "they").

1.5.7 Tokenization

This involves the process of breaking up the content into sentences and phrases. The work is breaking down a text into smaller chunks, or "tokens," while leaving out some characters, including punctuation.

Consider the following example:

Text input: Potter arrived having walked to school yesterday.

Potter went to school yesterday, according to the text output.

The fundamental flaw in this strategy is that it works better with some languages than others. This is especially true for tonal languages like Mandarin or Vietnamese.

Depending on how it is said, the Mandarin term "ma" can imply "a horse," "hemp," "a scold," or "a mother." The NLP algorithms are seriously at risk.

1.6 Algorithms and Models in NLP

Although NLP is a strong tool with many advantages, there are still a number of natural language processing constraints and issues:

- Contextual terminology
- Substitutes
- Irony and facetiousness
- Uncertainty
- Grammatical or pronunciation errors
- Colloquialisms and slang
- Specificity to the domain language
- Low-resource languages
- Lack of advancement and research.
- Contextual words and phrases and homonyms.

The same words and phrases can have different meanings depending on the context of a statement, and many terms, especially in English, have similar pronunciations but quite different meanings.

For example:

I ran to the store since we were out of milk.

Can I run something past you real quick?

It looks like the house is in bad shape or run down.

Since we are able to read the context of a statement and understand every definition, humans can readily understand these. Even if NLP language models have learned all of the meanings, it may still be challenging to tell them apart in context.

Homonyms, which are pairs of words that sound alike but mean different things, can present issues for speech-to-text and question-answering systems because they aren't written in text. Even for humans, using their and there incorrectly is a widespread issue.

1.6.1 Synonyms

Synonyms may present issues analogous to those related to contextual comprehension since we utilize a range of words to convey the same notion. Additionally, while some of these terms – like little, tiny, and minute – may all have the exact same meaning; others – like little, small, and minute – might have varying degrees of complexity. Moreover, different people use synonyms to denote somewhat different meanings within their own personal vocabularies.

Therefore, when creating NLP systems, it's essential to include all potential synonyms and definitions of words. Even while text analysis algorithms may occasionally make mistakes, they will get better at understanding synonyms as they receive more useful training data.

1.6.2 Irony and sarcasm

Irony and acerbity are forms of communication that involve expressing meanings that are different or opposite to what is literally stated. While they are often used in spoken and written language, they can pose challenges for natural language processing (NLP) systems due to their nuanced nature.

Irony refers to expressing a meaning that is opposite to the literal interpretation of the words used. For example, saying "What a beautiful day!" when it is actually raining heavily can be ironic. Irony relies on context, tone of voice, and understanding shared knowledge or expectations. Recognizing irony in text can be difficult for NLP systems because it requires understanding the underlying context and the discrepancy between the literal and intended meanings.

Sarcasm, on the other hand, involves using irony with an intention to mock, ridicule, or convey contempt. Sarcasm often relies on tone of voice and relies heavily on context and shared knowledge. In written text, sarcasm can be particularly challenging to detect because it lacks the accompanying vocal cues.

NLP systems have made progress in detecting and understanding irony and sarcasm, but it remains an ongoing research challenge. Some approaches involve analyzing linguistic patterns, sentiment analysis, context modelling, and leveraging large amounts of data to learn associations between specific phrases or expressions and their sarcastic or ironic meanings. However, due to the subtleties and subjectivity involved, accurately detecting and interpreting irony and sarcasm in text remains a complex task for NLP systems.

Overall, while NLP systems have made strides in understanding and processing language, the accurate detection and interpretation of irony and sarcasm still present significant challenges that researchers are actively working on.

1.6.3 Ambiguity

In NLP, sentences and phrases that have the potential for two or more meanings are referred to as ambiguous.

Lexical ambiguity: A term that can be used as an adjective, verb, or noun is said to have lexical ambiguity.

Semantic ambiguity: The interpretation of a statement depends on its context. For instance, I could see the boy on the beach with my binoculars. It's possible that the youngster was holding my binoculars or that I saw him through them.

Syntactic ambiguity: This obscures the prior statement's meaning. Both the verb "saw" and the noun "boy" can be modified by the adverb "with my binoculars."

This statement alone is challenging to understand without the context of the surrounding language, even for humans. One NLP solution that can, at least partially, fix the issue is POS (part of speech) tagging.

1.6.4 Errors in text and speech

Text analysis may be hampered by misspelled or improperly used terms. Although they can handle typical errors, autocorrect and grammar checkers frequently fail to comprehend the writer's purpose.

It might be challenging for a machine to understand spoken language due to mispronunciations, accent differences, stutters, etc. These problems can be reduced, though, as language databases expand and intelligent assistants are taught by their specific users.

1.6.5 Colloquialisms and slang

Specifically for models intended for a large audience, informal phrases, idioms, and cultural jargon provide a variety of difficulties for NLP. Since colloquialisms are not regarded as formal language, they may not even have a "dictionary definition," and they may even have different meanings depending on where you are. Additionally, new terminology emerge daily as cultural slang develops and changes.

Here, custom models may be trained and updated often, however doing so requires a lot of data.

1.6.6 Domain-specific language

It's possible that different businesses and industries utilize very different languages. An NLP processing model needed for processing legal papers, for example, would be very different from one needed for processing medical data. Despite the large number of analysis tools that are currently on the market that have been trained for specific disciplines, specialized businesses may still need to create or train their own models.

1.6.7 Low-resource languages

The most well-known, extensively used languages have seen the most development of AI machine learning NLP applications. It is simply amazing how much translation systems' accuracy has increased. However, many languages are regularly neglected and overlooked, especially those spoken by people with less access to technology. For instance, based on language vs. dialect, some estimates place the number of languages spoken worldwide at around 3000. Simply told, very little is known about many of these languages.

Recent methods, such as multilingual sentence embeddings and multilingual transformers (using BERT, or "bidirectional encoder representations from transformers" from Google), aim to identify and capitalize on the universal similarities that exist between languages.

1.6.8 Lack of research and development

Machine learning requires a LOT of data, billions of training data points, in order to function properly. As more data is used to train NLP models, they become more effective. Nevertheless, fresh data, customized algorithms, and machine learning techniques are always being created. Any of the aforementioned problems will require further research and innovative solutions.

Thanks to cutting-edge techniques like artificial neural networks and deep learning, many NLP strategies, algorithms, and models may operate gradually, like the human mind does. We may have solutions to some of these issues in the near future as they intensify and grow.

Many of the aforementioned NLP processing restrictions can be considerably reduced by using SaaS text analysis tools like MonkeyLearn, which enable users to train their own machine learning NLP models, frequently in just a few clicks. MonkeyLearn's no-code tools, which are tailored to the language and requirements of your company, offer significant NLP advantages for streamlining customer care procedures, discovering what consumers are saying about your company on social media, and closing the feedback loop with customers.

1.7 Introduction to the Natural Language Tool Kit (NLTK)

The NLTK (Natural Language Toolkit) is the primary Python API for NLP (natural language processing). It is a particularly effective tool for preparing text data for later analysis, such as using ML models. It helps convert words into numbers, which the model may make use of. An easy introduction to NLTK for beginners that also introduces Python begins with this part.

Programming language processing is effectively introduced by Python's natural language processing. It explains the fundamentals of creating Python programs, working with corpora, classifying text, analyzing linguistic structure, and more. The authors of NLTK wrote this article: https://www.nltk.org/install.html

Some simple things you can do with NLTK:

- Tokenize and tag some text
- Identify named entities
- Display a parse tree.

The Natural Language Toolkit provides a comprehensive set of tools and resources for working with human language data. The open-source software NLTK supports a number of NLP functions, including text preparation, tokenization, part-of-speech tagging, named entity recognition, sentiment analysis, and others.

1.7.1 Introduction to NLTK's features

1. **Tokenization:** NLTK provides tokenization functions to split text into words or sentences. It supports various tokenization methods, including word tokenization and sentence tokenization, which are fundamental steps in many NLP tasks.

2. **Text preprocessing:** NLTK offers functionalities for text preprocessing tasks, such includes deleting stop words, changing the text's case, and removing punctuation (common words like "the," "is," etc.), and performing stemming or lemmatization to normalize words.

3. **Part-of-speech (POS) tagging:** NLTK includes pre-trained models and functions for part-of-speech tagging, which contains labeling individually the word in a sentence with its corresponding grammatical or structural category (noun, verb, adjective, etc.). This information is crucial for many downstream NLP tasks.

4. **Named entity recognition (NER):** NLTK provides tools for termed entity recall, which involves identifying and classifying named entities (e.g., person names, locations, organizations) within text. This functionality is essential for tasks like information extraction and text understanding.

5. **Sentiment analysis:** NLTK includes built-in sentiment analysis capabilities, allowing users to perform sentiment classification on text data. It delivers pre-trained models and lexicons that can be utilized to determine the sentiment (positive, negative, neutral) expressed in a piece of text.

6. **Corpora and language resources:** NLTK offers a wide range of corpora and language resources for various languages. These resources include large groups of text data, including news articles, movie reviews, and more, which would be used for performing training and valuation of NLP models.

7. **Text classification:** NLTK provides tools for text classification tasks, such as document classification or spam detection. It includes algorithms like naïve Bayes, decision trees, and maximum entropy classifiers that can be trained on labeled data to classify text into predefined categories.

8. **Concordance and collocation:** NLTK provides functionalities to explore text data and discover patterns. It allows users to find occurrences of specific words within a text, examine their context (concordance), and identify frequent word combinations (collocations).

9. **WordNet:** NLTK integrates WordNet, a lexical database that provides access to synsets (sets of synonymous words) and their relationships, such as hypernyms (superordinate concepts) and

hyponyms (subordinate concepts). WordNet can be utilized for semantic analysis, term meaning clarification, and similarity calculations.

1.7.2 Conclusion

NLTK is a powerful and versatile library that offers an extensive variety of tools and resources for performing NLP tasks. It serves as an essential toolkit for beginners and researchers alike, offering a comprehensive set of functionalities to process, analyze, and understand human language data. With its vast array of features and easy-to-use interface, NLTK has become a go-to choice for many NLP practitioners and researchers in the Python ecosystem.

1.8 Case study: Sentiment analysis for product reviews

Introduction

In this case study, we will explore how natural language processing (NLP) techniques can be applied to accomplish sentiment analysis on product reviews. Determining the attitude or sentiment that is being portrayed in a text by performing a sentiment analysis can be valuable for businesses to understand customer feedback and make informed decisions.

Problem Statement

A company wants to analyze customer sentiments regarding their products by leveraging NLP. They have collected a large dataset of customer reviews for their products and want to advance a sentiment analysis system or structure that can automatically classify these reviews as neutral, adverse, or none.

Data Collection

The company has gathered a dataset consisting of thousands of customer reviews for their products. Each review is labeled with a sentiment category (positive, negative, or neutral). The dataset includes a variety of products, such as electronics, clothing, and home appliances.

Data Preprocessing

The raw text data needs to be preprocessed before applying NLP techniques. Preprocessing steps may involve tokenization (breaking text into words or sentences), removing punctuation and stop words, converting all characters to lowercase, and applying stemming or lemmatization to reduce words to their base form.

Feature Extraction

To analyze the sentiment in the reviews, we need to convert the words into numerical features that can be used by machine learning algorithms. Techniques like bag-of-words or TF-IDF could be applied to produce feature depictions of the text data.

Model Training and Evaluation

Once the features are extracted, the tagged reviews can be used to train a machine learning model. Popular algorithms like naïve Bayes, support vector machines (SVMs), or more advanced models like recurrent neural networks (RNNs) or transformer-based models can be used for classification. For model evaluation, the dataset can be divided into training and testing sets, and performance metrics such as accuracy, precision, recall, and F1 score can be computed.

Model Deployment

After training and assessing the model, it can be deployed in order to classify sentiments in real-time. The company can develop an application or integrate the model into their existing system to process customer reviews and provide sentiment analysis results.

Continuous Improvement

To increase the sentiment analysis system's effectiveness, the model can be fine-tuned by integrating user feedback. The company can collect additional labeled data from users and periodically retrain the model to make it more accurate and robust.

Conclusion

This case study demonstrates how sentiment analysis in product reviews may be done using NLP techniques. By employing machine learning models to better understand customer sentiment, identify areas for improvement, and make data-driven decisions, businesses may enhance their goods and services. Sentiment analysis is only one example of how NLP may be used to extract crucial information from text data in a number of settings and applications.

2

Parsing and Syntax

Examining a string of symbols that follow the rules of formal grammar, whether they are in natural language, computer languages, or data structures, is known as parsing, syntax analysis, or syntactic analysis. The Latin term "pars" (orationis), which refers to a segment of speech, is where the word "parsing" originates.

The term has a few slightly different interpretations in linguistics and computer science. To ascertain the specific meaning of a sentence or word, traditional sentence parsing is typically utilized, maybe with the aid of tools like sentence diagrams. Usually, emphasis is placed on the importance of grammatical divisions like subject and predicate.

In computational linguistics, the phrase refers to the formal breakdown of a sentence or other string of words by a computer into its constituent parts, creating a parse tree indicating their syntactic relationship to each other and perhaps also carrying semantic and other information (p-values). A parse forest or set of parse trees may be produced by various parsing algorithms given a syntactically ambiguous input [4].

The phrase is also used to describe language comprehension in psycholinguistics. In this meaning, parsing refers to the analysis of a sentence or phrase (in spoken language or text) "in terms of grammatical constituents, identifying the parts of speech, syntactic relations, etc." This expression is often used to describe the linguistic cues that allow speakers to comprehend sentences from the garden path.

The practice of separating input code into its individual syntactic parts to make it simpler to create compilers and interpreters is referred to as decomposition in computer science. The phrase can also be used to describe a divide or separation.

2.1 Word-level Analysis

This basically adheres to the morpheme ordering principle. In another sense, the model makes it clear which morpheme classes can follow one another in a word. For instance, in English, the plural morpheme normally follows the noun rather than coming before it.

Word-level analysis is an essential activity in natural language processing (NLP), where the main objective is to analyze and extract meaningful information from individual words in a given text. It involves various techniques and methods to process and analyze words in order to gain insights into their characteristics, relationships, and usage within the context of a particular language or text.

Here are some common word-level analysis tasks in NLP:

1. **Tokenization:** Tokenization is the division of a text into tokens, or individual words. It helps in breaking down the text into meaningful units that can be further processed and analyzed.
2. **Part-of-speech (POS) tagging:** POS tagging involves assigning a grammatical category (e.g., noun, verb, adjective) to every single word in a sentence. It provides information about the role and function of words within a sentence, aiding in syntactic analysis and language understanding.
3. **Lemmatization:** Lemmatization is a technique for removing meaning from words to their base or canonical form, known as lemmas. It helps in normalizing variations of words and reducing inflectional forms to their dictionary representation. For example, lemmatizing the word "running" would result in the lemma "run."
4. **Stemming:** Stemming is similar to lemmatization in that it aims to reduce words to their base form. However, stemming typically involves heuristic-based approaches that remove prefixes or suffixes from words to obtain the root form (stem). Stemming may result in non-dictionary words, unlike lemmatization. For instance, stemming the word "running" may produce the stem "runn."
5. **Named entity recognition (NER):** In a given text, NER locates and categorizes named entities like names of people, places, businesses, events, and more. It helps in extracting structured information and understanding the context of a text.
6. **Word sense disambiguation:** The practice of identifying the intended meaning of a word with several meanings based on its context is known as word sense disambiguation. It involves resolving word ambiguities to ensure accurate understanding and interpretation.

7. **Word frequency analysis:** Word frequency analysis involves including the occurrence of words in a text corpus. It helps in identifying the most frequent words, which can be helpful for tasks including text summarization, keyword extraction, and language modeling.

8. **Word embeddings:** Dense vector representations called word embeddings show the relationships between words in sentences. Techniques like word2vec and GloVe create word embeddings by training on large corpora. These embeddings enable various downstream responsibilities, such as similarity calculation, term analogy, and document classification.

These are just a few examples of word-level analysis tasks in NLP. Each task serves a different purpose and contributes to understanding the properties and characteristics of words within a text or language. Researchers and practitioners employ these techniques to build robust NLP models and applications capable of understanding, generating, and processing human language.

2.2 Utilizing Regular Expressions

Regular expressions (regex) are powerful tools used in computer science and programming to match and manipulate text patterns. They provide a concise and flexible way to search, extract, and manipulate text data based on specific patterns and rules.

Here are some key components and concepts related to regular expressions:

1. **Metacharacters:** Metacharacters are special characters that have a symbolic meaning in regular expressions. Examples include:

    -   . (dot): Any single character, excluding newlines, is matched.
    -   ∧ (caret): The beginning of the line is being matched.
    -   $ (dollar): Matches the line's end.
    -   * (asterisk): Matches zero or further occurrences of the previous character or group.
    -   + (plus): Matches one or more instances of the character or group before it.
    -   ? (question mark): Matches 0 or 1 instances of the character or group before it.
    -   [...] (character class): The character within the brackets is being matched.
    -   | (pipe): Matches either the expression before or after it and functions as an OR operator.

2. **Character classes:** You can match a certain group of characters using character classes. Character class patterns that are frequent include:

- [0-9]: Any digit from 0 to 9 matches.
- [a-z]: Any lowercase letter from a through z matches.
- [A-Z]: Any uppercase letter from A to Z matches.
- [a-z A-Z]: Any letter matches (case is irrelevant).
- [∧a-z]: Any character that isn't a lowercase letter gets matched.

3. **Quantifiers:** Quantifiers define the number of occurrences of a character or group. Some commonly used quantifiers are:

- *: Matches zero or more occurrences.
- +: Matches one or more than one occurrences.
- ?: Matches zero or more than one occurrence.
- {n}: The matches are exactly n occurrences.
- {n,}: The matches at least n occurrences.
- {n,m}: Matches at least n and at most m occurrences.

4. **Grouping and capturing:** Parentheses ( ) are used for grouping and capturing parts of the matched text. They also allow applying quantifiers and other operators to a group of characters.

5. **Anchors:** Anchors are used to match specific positions within the text. The ∧ anchor the beginning of a line, and the $ anchor matches the line's end.

6. **Backreferences:** Backreferences refer to previously matched groups in a regular expression. They allow you to match the same text that was matched by a previous group.

7. **Escape characters:** Some characters have a special meaning in regular expressions, but if you want to match them literally, you need to provide them with a backslash (\). For example, to match a literal dot (.), you would use \.

Regular expressions are supported in many programming languages and text editors, such as Python, JavaScript, Java, Perl, and more. They are versatile and extensively used for responsibilities such as text search and auxiliary, data validation, parsing, and text preprocessing in various applications. However, constructing complex regular expressions can be challenging, so it's often helpful to refer to documentation and practice with examples to master their usage [5].

A regular expression (RE) language can be used to specify text search strings. RE helps us match or find other strings or collections of strings by making use of a certain syntax that is stored in a pattern. Similar to how UNIX and MS WORD employ regular expressions to search text. Many different search engines use the RE features.

The following are some of the crucial characteristics of RE.

Stephen Cole Kleene, American Mathematician, formalized the regular expression language.

Regular expression (RE) is a formula in a specific language that can be used for identifying basic classes of strings, a series of symbols. In other words, we can say that RE is an algebraic notation for characterizing a set of strings.

Regular expression involves two components, one being the pattern that we wish to search for and the other being a corpus of text from which we need to search, therefore we may say that RE is an algebraic notation for characterizing a set of strings.

Mathematically, a regular expression can be defined as follows:

- ε is a regular expression that denotes that the language has an empty string, as shown by the symbol.
- φ is an empty language, as indicated by the regular expression.

If X and Y are regular expressions, then

X, Y

X.Y (concatenation of XY)

X+Y (union of X and Y)

X*, Y* (Kleene closure of X and Y)

are also regular expressions.

If a string is created using the aforementioned guidelines, then that string is also a regular expression

2.3 Normalization of Text

A pre-processing technique called text normalization aims to enhance the text's quality and prepare it for machine processing. Case normalization, tokenization, stop word elimination, parts-of-speech (POS) labeling, and stemming are the four key phases in text normalization.

Case normalization affects languages that use both capital and lowercase letters. All languages that employ the Latin or Cyrillic alphabets, including Russian, Mongolian, and others, use both upper and lowercase letters. Occasionally, the term is also used in other languages like Greek, Armenian, Cherokee, and Coptic. Letters are all transformed to the same case when they are normalized.

It is extremely helpful in semantic use situations. This may hinder performance in other situations. Spam messages may contain more words in all uppercase than ordinary mail.

Another usual normalization step is the elimination of punctuation from the text. Again, this may or may not be useful depending on the situation. In the majority of cases, this should result in favorable outcomes. However, in certain situations, such as spam or grammatical models, it might reduce performance. Exclamation marks and other punctuation are more frequently used to emphasize points in spam emails.

Text normalization, also known as text pre-processing, is the process of transforming raw textual data into a standardized and consistent format. It involves applying a series of rules and techniques to prepare the text for further analysis, modelling, or other natural language processing (NLP) tasks. Text normalization helps to reduce noise, improve accuracy, and ensure better understanding and processing of the text [6].

Here are some common techniques used in text normalization:

1. **Lowercasing:** Converting all characters in the text to lowercase. This helps in treating uppercase and lowercase versions of the same word as identical.
2. **Tokenization:** Splitting the text into distinct words or tokens. This step is vital for further analysis and processing.
3. **Removing punctuation:** The deletion of punctuation, including commas, periods, exclamation points, and question marks. This simplifies the text and eliminates unnecessary noise.
4. **Removing special characters:** Removing special characters that do not convey significant meaning, such as symbols, emojis, or non-alphanumeric characters.
5. **Removing stop words:** The stop words are common lexical items with little semantic content, such as "the," "is," "and," etc. Removing stop words can reduce noise and improve the efficiency of text processing.
6. **Lemmatization:** Transforming words into their lemma, or fundamental or canonical form. This involves eliminating inflections and suffixes, and converting words to their dictionary form. For example, lemmatizing "running" would result in the lemma "run."
7. **Stemming:** Stemming is a simpler technique compared to lemmatization. It involves removing prefixes or suffixes from words to obtain the word's root form (stem). However, stemming may produce non-dictionary words. For instance, stemming the word "running" may result in the stem "runn."
8. **Spell correction:** Correcting misspelled words based on known dictionaries or statistical methods. This helps in improving text quality and reducing ambiguity [7].
9. **Handling contractions:** Expanding contractions like "can't" to "cannot," "don't" to "do not," etc., to ensure consistent representation and better analysis.

10. **Normalizing numbers:** Converting numbers to a standardized format. For example, converting "1,000" to "1000" or replacing numbers with a generic token like "#NUM#" to treat all numbers uniformly.

Text normalization is typically performed as a pre-processing step before feeding the text into models or algorithms for tasks like sentiment analysis, text classification, machine conversion, information retrieval, and more. The specific techniques employed may vary depending on the demands of the assignment and the characteristics of the text data being processed.

2.4 Edit Distance Computation

Given two character strings s_1 and s_2, the edit distance between them is the minimum number of edit operations required to transform s_1 into s_2 . Most commonly, the edit operations allowed for this purpose are: (i) inserting a character into a string, (ii) deleting a character from a string, and (iii) replacing a character in a string with another character. This measure is also referred to as Levenshtein distance. For instance, the edit distance between "cat" and "dog" is 3, representing the need for three operations to transform one into the other.

In some cases, the concept of edit distance can be extended to account for varying weights associated with different types of edit operations. For example, assigning a higher weight to replacing a character "s" with "p" compared to replacing it with "a" due to their keyboard proximity. This weight-based approach can be particularly effective in practical scenarios. However, our current discussion will primarily concentrate on the scenario where all edit operations carry equal weight [10].

The edit distance, or the Levenshtein distance, serves as a metric to quantify the dissimilarity between two strings. It gauges the minimal number of actions necessary to convert one string to another by applying insertions, deletions, or substitutions of individual characters. The operations allowed in edit distance are:

1. Insertion: Adding a character to one of the strings.
2. Deletion: Removing a character from one of the strings.
3. Substitution: Replacing a character in one string with another.

The edit distance between two strings is computed by finding the minimum number of these operations required to transform one string into the other.

For example, let's calculate the edit distance between the words "kitten" and "sitting":

1. "kitten" → "sitten" (substitute "s" for "k")
2. "sitten" → "sittin" (substitute "I" for "e")
3. "sittin" → "sitting" (insert "g").

In this case, three operations were needed to transform "kitten" into "sitting," so the edit distance is 3.

Edit distance has various applications, such as:

1. **Spelling correction:** Finding the closest matching word to a misspelled word based on edit distance.
2. **DNA sequence alignment:** Measuring the similarity between DNA sequences.
3. **Natural language processing:** Identifying similar words or finding the closest matching phrase in text.

The concept of edit distance is fundamental in computational linguistics and has several variations and optimizations. It allows for comparing and quantifying the similarity or dissimilarity between strings, which can be useful in a wide range of applications.

2.4.1 Edit distance calculation with example

The edit distance, commonly referred to as the Levenshtein distance, is a metric used to quantify the dissimilarity between two character strings. It signifies the smallest count of operations—such as insertions, deletions, or substitutions—needed to convert one string into the other [11].

For example, consider the two strings "cat" and "cut." The edit distance between these strings is 1, as we can transform "cat" into "cut" by replacing the "a" with a "u."

The edit distance can be calculated recursively using dynamic programming. Let the two input strings be s and t, and let M[i,j] denote the edit distance between the first i characters of s and the first j characters of t. The edit distance can then be calculated as follows:

- M[i, j] = 0 if i = 0 and j = 0 (i.e., both strings are empty)
- M[i, j] = i if j = 0 (i.e., t is empty)
- M[i, j] = j if i = 0 (i.e., s is empty)
- M[i, j] = M[i−1,j−1] if s[i] = t[j] (i.e., the characters are the same)
- M[i, j] = min(M[i−1,j], M[i,j−1], M[i−1,j−1]) + 1 otherwise (i.e., the characters are different).

The last case represents the minimum number of operations required to transform s into t. The three possible operations are:

- Insert a character into s to match the character at position j in t.
- Delete a character from s to ignore the character at position i.
- Substitute the character at position i in s with the character at position j in t.

The edit distance has various applications in natural language processing, including spell checking, word suggestion, machine translation, and more. It is also used in bioinformatics to compare DNA and protein sequences.

Sure! Let's calculate the edit distance between two example strings, "kitten" and "sitting," using the Levenshtein distance algorithm.

Step 1: Create a matrix with dimensions $(7 + 1) \times (6 + 1)$:

```
|   | s | i | t | t | i | n | g |
|---|---|---|---|---|---|---|---|
| k |   |   |   |   |   |   |   |
| i |   |   |   |   |   |   |   |
| t |   |   |   |   |   |   |   |
| t |   |   |   |   |   |   |   |
| e |   |   |   |   |   |   |   |
| n |   |   |   |   |   |   |   |
|   |   |   |   |   |   |   |   |
```

Step 2: Initialize the first row and the first column:

```
|   | s | i | t | t | i | n | g |
|---|---|---|---|---|---|---|---|
| k | 0 | 1 | 2 | 3 | 4 | 5 | 6 |
| i |   |   |   |   |   |   |   |
| t |   |   |   |   |   |   |   |
| t |   |   |   |   |   |   |   |
| e |   |   |   |   |   |   |   |
| n |   |   |   |   |   |   |   |
|   |   |   |   |   |   |   |   |
```

Step 3: Iterate through the matrix, calculating the minimum edit distance for each cell:

For cell (1,1), the characters "k" and "s" are different. We choose the minimum value among the left neighbor (0), the upper neighbor (1), and the diagonal neighbor (0) and add 1. The minimum value is 0, so we update cell (1,1) to 0.

```
|   | s | i | t | t | i | n | g |
|---|---|---|---|---|---|---|---|
| k | 0 | 1 | 2 | 3 | 4 | 5 | 6 |
| i | 1 |   |   |   |   |   |   |
| t |   |   |   |   |   |   |   |
| t |   |   |   |   |   |   |   |
| e |   |   |   |   |   |   |   |
| n |   |   |   |   |   |   |   |
|   |   |   |   |   |   |   |   |
```

Continue this process for the remaining cells:

Step 4: The value in the bottom-right cell (6, 7) represents the minimum edit distance, which is 2. Therefore, the edit distance between "kitten" and "sitting" is 2.

```
|     | s | i | t | t | i | n | g |
|-----|---|---|---|---|---|---|---|
| k   | 0 | 1 | 2 | 3 | 4 | 5 | 6 |
| i   | 1 | 1 | 2 | 3 | 4 | 5 | 6 |
| t   | 2 | 2 | 1 | 2 | 3 | 4 | 5 |
| t   | 3 | 3 | 2 | 1 | 2 | 3 | 4 |
| e   | 4 | 4 | 3 | 2 | 2 | 3 | 4 |
| n   | 5 | 5 | 4 | 3 | 3 | 2 | 3 |
|     | 6 | 6 | 5 | 4 | 4 | 3 | 2 |
```

To visualize the edits needed to transform "kitten" into "sitting," you can trace back through the matrix from the bottom-right cell to the top-left cell, choosing the path with the smallest values in each step. The path represents the minimum sequence of operations (insertions, deletions, or substitutions) required.

In this case, the path is:

$$(6,7) \rightarrow (5,6) \rightarrow (4,5) \rightarrow (3,4) \rightarrow (2,3) \rightarrow (1,2) \rightarrow (1,1) \rightarrow (0,0)$$

This path corresponds to the operations: substitution of "k" with "s", substitution of "e" with """". Hence, the minimum edit distance of 2 indicates that two substitutions are required to transform "kitten" into "sitting."

I hope this example helps illustrate how the edit distance is calculated using the Levenshtein distance algorithm.

2.5 Parsing and Syntax–Spelling Relations

A natural language parser functions as a software tool that identifies coherent word groups (known as "phrases") and determines the roles of words within a sentence, such as subjects or objects of verbs. This parsing process involves breaking down a text into smaller segments based on grammar rules. In instances where a sentence cannot be parsed, it might be indicative of grammatical errors.

The parser's operation commences with identifying the sentence's subject. As it dissects the text sequence, the parser groups words that exhibit a certain phrase-like relationship. These groups of interconnected words constitute what we commonly refer to as the subject. The parsing process relies on syntactic structures and parts of speech, adhering to context-free grammar rules that are concerned with word arrangement rather than contextual nuances. It's essential to highlight that the grammar adheres to syntax rules but might lack contextual coherence.

It seems there might be a slight confusion in your question. Parsing and syntax are related to the analysis and structure of sentences or programming code, while spelling refers to the correct arrangement of letters in words. I'll provide an explanation for both:

1. **Parsing and syntax:** Parsing is the process of analyzing the grammatical construction of a ruling to determine its syntactic components and their relationships. It involves breaking down a sentence into its constituent parts (such as nouns, verbs, phrases) and understanding the hierarchical relationships between them.

   Syntax, on the other hand, relates to the rubrics and values that govern the arrangement of words and phrases to create grammatically correct sentences. It defines the structure and order in which words and phrases can be combined to convey meaning.

   The process of parsing and analyzing syntax involves methods such as part-of-speech tagging, dependency parsing, and constituency parsing. These techniques use linguistic rules and statistical models to identify and analyze the grammatical structure of sentences.

2. **Spelling:** Spelling relates to the correct arrangement of letters in words. It ensures that words are written accurately according to the standard conventions of a given language. Proper spelling is crucial for effective communication and understanding.

   In the framework of natural language processing (NLP) or computational linguistics, spelling correction or spell checking is a common task. It involves identifying and correcting misspelled words in text. Spell checking algorithms typically use dictionaries or language models to suggest corrections for misspelled words based on their similarity to correctly spelled words.

   Spell checking can be performed using techniques such as Levenshtein distance, which measures the edit distance between words to find the most similar options. Language models can also be employed to suggest the most probable correction based on the setting of the adjacent words.

   Overall, parsing and syntax analysis focuses on the structure and relationships within sentences, while spelling ensures the accurate representation of words by adhering to correct letter arrangements. Both aspects are important in language processing and play distinct roles in understanding and manipulating textual data.

2.6 Error Detection and Correction

Grammatical error correction (GEC) involves rectifying various types of errors in text, including spelling, punctuation, grammar, and word choice errors.

Typically, GEC is framed as a task focused on sentence correction. A GEC system takes a possibly flawed sentence as input and is tasked with converting it into a corrected version. Consider the following example:

Input (flawed): She see Tom is catched by policeman in park at last night.

Output (corrected): She saw Tom caught by a policeman in the park last night.

One of the most extensively employed applications of NLP is spell checking. This task serves a wide array of purposes such as information retrieval, proof-reading, and email clients. Presently, spell checkers find utility in numerous NLP applications. They function as linguistic tools that dissect text for spelling errors, signaling the presence of misspelled or unintended words. Errors in typing can be classified into two categories: "non-word errors" and "real-word errors".

Error detection and correction in natural language processing (NLP) includes classifying and rectifying errors in text, such as spelling mistakes, grammatical errors, and contextual inconsistencies. It aims to improve the accuracy and quality of textual data for various NLP applications.

Here are some common techniques and approaches used for error detection and correction in NLP:

1. **Spell checking:** Spell checking algorithms identify and correct misspelled words by comparing them against a dictionary or language model. They use techniques like Levenshtein distance or phonetic similarity to suggest alternative corrections.
2. **Grammar checking:** Grammar checking focuses on identifying and correcting grammatical errors in text, such as incorrect verb forms, subject-verb agreement, and sentence structure. This is often completed by means of rule-based approaches or statistical models that capture grammar patterns.
3. **Named entity recognition (NER):** NER identifies and classifies named entities in text, such as person names, organization names, locations, etc. It helps in detecting and correcting errors related to the identification and classification of named entities.
4. **Contextual analysis:** Contextual analysis involves understanding the import and setting of words and phrases in a given text. By considering the surrounding words and their relationships, contextual analysis techniques can help detect and correct errors that arise due to word ambiguity or incorrect word usage.

5. **Machine translation:** Machine translation systems can be used for error detection and correction by decoding text from one language to another and comparing the translations. Inconsistent or nonsensical translations can indicate errors in the original text.

6. **Language models:** Language models, such as N-gram models or neural language representations, can be skilled on large volumes of text data to capture the statistical patterns of language. These models can help detect errors by identifying improbable or ungrammatical word sequences.

7. **Rule-based approaches:** Rule-based methods use handcrafted linguistic rules to detect and correct errors. These rules are designed based on language-specific grammar rules and patterns. Rule-based approaches are effective for detecting specific types of errors but may not handle all possible cases.

8. **Machine learning approaches:** Machine learning methods, such as supervised or unsupervised learning, can be applied to error detection and correction. Models can be trained on annotated or parallel data to learn patterns and make predictions for error correction.

It's important to note that error detection and correction in NLP can be challenging due to the complexities of natural language and the ambiguity that exists in text. Therefore, a combination of different techniques and approaches is often employed to achieve better accuracy and coverage in error detection and correction tasks.

2.7 Words and their Classes

Contemporary grammatical frameworks generally categorize words into four primary classes (verbs, nouns, adjectives, adverbs) and five additional classes (determiners, prepositions, pronouns, conjunctions, interjections), resulting in a total of nine word classes (or parts of speech). It's worth noting that certain grammarians might employ alternative systems, leading to recognition of either eight or ten distinct word classes.

Verbs: Verbs denote actions or states, such as run, work, study, be, seem.

Nouns: Nouns pertain to entities like people, places, or things, such as mother, town, Rome, car, dog.

Adjectives: Adjectives describe nouns and convey characteristics, like kind, clever, expensive.

Adverbs: Adverbs modify verbs, adjectives, or other adverbs, such as quickly, back, ever, badly, away, generally, completely.

Prepositions: Prepositions typically precede nouns or pronouns and indicate relationships with other words or elements, for instance after, down, near, of, plus, round, to.

Pronouns: Pronouns replace nouns, like me, you, his, it, this, that, mine, yours, who, what.

Interjections: Interjections lack grammatical significance and include words like ah, hey, oh, ouch, um, well.

Prefixes: Prefixes, such as non-, inter-, post-, are attached to words as in non-existent, interstellar, post-war.

Suffixes: Suffixes like -ation, -al, -ize are affixed to words, as seen in creation, national, prioritize.

Words with combining forms: Collections of words beginning with the combining forms mono- and poly-, such as monologue, polygraph.

Contractions: Abbreviated forms of words or phrases, often used in speech, like I'm, aren't, here's, gonna.

WH words: Interrogative words used to form questions, such as who, what, how.

In natural language processing (NLP), words stay as the fundamental units of language. They represent the smallest meaningful units of text that carry information and contribute to the overall meaning of sentences and documents. Words are typically identified by tokenization, which is the development of splitting text into separate arguments or tokens.

Word classes, also known as parts of speech, are groups that classify words based on their grammatical roles and behavior in sentences. Word classes help in understanding the syntactic structure and meaning of sentences. Some common word classes include:

1. **Nouns:** Nouns are words that represent people, places, things, or concepts. They can be concrete (e.g., "cat," "house") or abstract (e.g., "love," "happiness").
2. **Verbs:** Verbs denote actions, states, or occurrences. They describe what a subject does or the state it is in. Examples include "run," "eat," "sleep."
3. **Adjectives:** Adjectives adapt nouns or pronouns, provided that additional data about their qualities or attributes. Examples include "happy," "big," "red."

4. **Adverbs:** Adverbs modify verbs, adjectives, or other adverbs, indicating the manner, time, place, or degree of an action or quality. Examples include "quickly," "very," "often."

5. **Pronouns:** Pronouns are words used in place of nouns to refer to people, objects, or ideas. Examples include "he," "she," "it," "they."

6. **Prepositions:** Prepositions establish relationships between nouns (or pronouns) and other arguments in a sentence. They indicate location, time, direction, or manner. Examples include "in," "on," "at," "from."

7. **Conjunctions:** Conjunctions connect words, phrases, or clauses in a sentence. They can express coordination ("and," "but") or subordination ("if," "because").

8. **Determiners:** Determiners precede and modify nouns, indicating specificity, quantity, or possession. Examples include "the," "a," "some," "my."

9. **Interjections**: Interjections are words or phrases used to express emotions, surprise, or strong reactions. Examples include "oh," "wow," "ouch," "hey."

These word classes provide a basic framework for understanding the syntactic structure and grammatical properties of sentences. NLP methods, such as part-of-speech tagging, aim to automatically assign word classes to each word in a sentence, enabling deeper linguistic analysis and enabling various NLP applications, such as text generation, data removal, and sentiment analysis.

2.8 Part of Speech Tagging

Part of speech tagging is the process of transforming a sentence into various formats, such as a list of words or a list of tuples, where each tuple contains a word along with its corresponding part-of-speech tag. This tag indicates whether the word functions as a noun, adjective, verb, and so forth.

Tagging can be viewed as a form of classification, involving the automated assignment of descriptors to tokens. In this context, the descriptor is termed a "tag," which could represent a part-of-speech category, semantic information, and more.

Now, focusing on part-of-speech (PoS) tagging, it can be defined as the act of allocating a specific part of speech to a given word. Commonly referred to as POS tagging, it's essentially the task of labelling every word within a sentence with its appropriate part of speech. As a reminder, parts of speech encompass nouns, verbs, adverbs, adjectives, pronouns, conjunctions, along with their subcategories.

The practice of POS tagging is generally categorized into rule-based POS tagging, stochastic POS tagging, and transformation-based tagging.

Part-of-speech tagging (POS tagging) holds significant importance in the realm of natural language processing (NLP). This foundational task involves attributing grammatical categories or part-of-speech labels to individual words within a sentence. The process aids in comprehending the syntactic structure of sentences and plays a pivotal role in numerous NLP applications like machine translation, information extraction, sentiment analysis, and text generation.

The process of POS tagging involves using computational models, such as rule-based systems, statistical models, or machine learning algorithms, to automatically assign the appropriate part-of-speech tag to each term in a sentence. These tags indicate the word's syntactic role and behavior in the sentence.

Here's an example of POS tagging for the sentence: "The cat is sitting on the mat."

```
|   |  s  |  i  |  t  |  t  |  i  |  n  |  g  |
|---|---|---|---|---|---|---|---|
| k | 0 | 1 | 2 | 3 | 4 | 5 | 6 |
| i | 1 | 1 | 2 | 3 | 4 | 5 | 6 |
| t | 2 | 2 | 1 | 2 | 3 | 4 | 5 |
| t | 3 | 3 | 2 | 1 | 2 | 3 | 4 |
| e | 4 | 4 | 3 | 2 | 2 | 3 | 4 |
| n | 5 | 5 | 4 | 3 | 3 | 2 | 3 |
|   | 6 | 6 | 5 | 4 | 4 | 3 | 2 |
```

In this example, each word in the sentence is assigned a part-of-speech tag:

- "The" and "the" are determiners.
- "cat" and "mat" are nouns.
- "is" and "sitting" are verbs.
- "on" is a preposition.
- "." is a punctuation mark.

There are numerous methods of POS tagging:

1. **Rule-based tagging:** Rule-based systems use handcrafted linguistic rules and patterns to assign POS tags based on word morphology, context, and syntactic rules. These rules may consider word suffixes, prefixes, surrounding words, and grammar patterns.

2. **Statistical tagging:** Statistical models use probabilistic techniques to learn the mapping between words and their corresponding POS tags from annotated training data. Hidden Markov models (HMMs) and conditional random fields (CRFs) are commonly used statistical models for POS tagging.

3. **Machine learning tagging:** Machine learning approaches use various algorithms, such as decision trees, support vector machines (SVM), or neural networks, to learn the patterns and associations between words and POS tags from annotated training data.

4. **Hybrid approaches:** Hybrid models combine rule-based, statistical, and machine learning techniques to recover POS tagging correctness. These models leverage the strengths of different approaches to achieve better results.

The choice of POS tagging approach depends on factors such as available resources, size and quality of training data, and specific requirements of the application.

POS tagging is a crucial step in NLP pipelines as it provides valuable syntactic information about words, enabling deeper linguistic analysis and facilitating downstream NLP tasks that rely on understanding the grammatical structure of sentences.

2.9 Sentiment Classification with Naïve Bayes: Case Study

Naïve Bayes stands as the most uncomplicated and swiftest classification algorithm, highly suitable for handling substantial volumes of data. Its effectiveness is evident across various applications such as spam filtering, text classification, sentiment analysis, and recommendation systems. The naïve Bayes classifier has proven its mettle in these contexts, leveraging the principles of the Bayes' probability theorem for making predictions on unknown classes.

Within the realm of machine learning, the naïve Bayes classification technique emerges as both straightforward and potent. It operates on the foundation of the Bayes theorem, adopting a crucial assumption of independence among features. This assumption is particularly strong when applying naïve Bayes classification to textual data analysis, as observed in natural language processing tasks, yielding commendable outcomes.

Alternate terms for naïve Bayes models include simple Bayes or independent Bayes models. Each of these designations refers to the classifier's decision-making rule grounded in the Bayes theorem. In practice, the naïve Bayes classifier effectively employs the Bayes theorem. By harnessing this classifier, the power of the Bayes theorem is harnessed for machine learning applications.

The Bayes theorem is pivotal in computing the probability of a hypothesis, especially when prior knowledge is accessible. It draws upon conditional probabilities to make these determinations. The formula underlying Bayes' theorem is provided below:

$$P(A \mid B) = P(B \mid A)^*P(A)/P(B)$$

In the context of the Bayes theorem, the term $P(A|B)$ denotes the posterior probability, which signifies the probability of a particular hypothesis A occurring given that event B has taken place. On the other hand, $P(B|A)$ represents the likelihood probability, indicating the probability of the observed evidence happening under the assumption that hypothesis A is true. The factor $P(A)$ stands as the prior probability, denoting the likelihood of the hypothesis before any evidence is considered. Lastly, $P(B)$ corresponds to the marginal probability, representing the overall probability associated with the observed evidence.

Sure! Let's walk through a case study on sentiment classification using naive Bayes.

2.9.1 Case study: Sentiment classification

Problem Statement

We want to build a sentiment classifier that can control the sentiment (positive or negative) of customer reviews for a product. The goal is to automatically classify new customer reviews based on their sentiment.

Dataset

We have a labeled dataset of customer reviews, where each assessment is considered as either positive or negative. The dataset contains a collection of text reviews along with their corresponding sentiment labels.

Approach

Step 1: Data preparation

- Load the dataset and initiate necessary preprocessing steps, including the elimination of punctuation, conversion of text to lowercase, and handling of stopwords.
- Partition the dataset into training and testing subsets.

Step 2: Feature generation

- Transform the textual reviews into numerical feature vectors compatible with the naive Bayes classifier.
- One prevalent strategy involves utilizing the bag-of-words model, where each review is converted into a vector reflecting word frequencies.
- Implement techniques like TF-IDF (term frequency-inverse document frequency) to allocate significance weights to words.

Step 3: Training the naïve Bayes classifier

- Train a naïve Bayes classifier using the training data.
- The naïve Bayes classifier operates under the assumption that features (words, in this case) exhibit conditional independence given the class (positive or negative sentiment).
- Compute the prior probabilities for each class (positive and negative) based on the training dataset.
- Estimate the likelihood probabilities for each word, considering the associated class.

Step 4: Sentiment categorization

- Employ the trained naïve Bayes classifier to classify novel, unseen customer reviews.
- Convert the content of the new review into the same feature vector format used during training.
- Determine the posterior probabilities for both class options (positive and negative) by utilizing the feature vector and the previously derived probabilities.
- Assign the sentiment classification for the review based on the class label linked to the higher probability.

Step 5: Performance assessment

- Evaluate the effectiveness of the sentiment classifier using the designated testing set.
- Compute performance metrics like accuracy, precision, recall, and F1-score to gauge the model's proficiency.

- Analyze instances of misclassification or areas where the model might encounter challenges.

Step 6: Model refinement

- Iterate on the model to improve its performance.
- Experiment with different preprocessing techniques, feature extraction methods, or other classification algorithms.
- Tune hyperparameters to find the best configuration for the classifier.

Conclusion

In this case study, we built a sentiment classifier using naïve Bayes for customer reviews. We followed the steps of data preprocessing, feature extraction, training the classifier, sentiment classification, and evaluation. The model's performance on the testing set can guide us in making improvements or refining the model further.

Naïve Bayes, a classification algorithm frequently employed in natural language processing (NLP), finds particular utility in tasks like sentiment classification. The primary objective of sentiment classification is to ascertain the sentiment of text content, such as movie reviews or social media posts, categorizing them as positive, negative, or neutral. In this case study, our focus lies in applying the naïve Bayes algorithm for sentiment classification on movie reviews.

Dataset: We will utilize the IMDb dataset, containing 50,000 movie reviews labeled as positive or negative. The dataset is divided into two equal halves: 25,000 reviews for training and an equal number for testing. Each review is preprocessed and represented as a bag-of-words structure, wherein every word in the review is converted into a feature.

Preprocessing: Preliminary to implementing the naïve Bayes algorithm, the data must undergo preprocessing. This entails converting the bag-of-words representation of each review into a numerical vector suitable for algorithm input. To accomplish this, the Count Vectorizer class from the scikit-learn library will be utilized.

Training : Subsequently, the training phase involves training a naïve Bayes classifier with the provided training data. The MultinomialNB class from scikit-learn, designed for classification with discrete features like word counts, will be utilized. The classifier will be fitted to the training data using the fit method.

Testing: Following classifier training, it will be evaluated on the testing data. The predict method will be employed to generate predictions for each review within the testing data. These predictions will then be juxtaposed with the true labels to gauge the classifier's performance. Evaluation metrics including accuracy, precision, and recall will be employed for performance measurement.

Results: Post-testing, performance evaluation will encompass metrics such as accuracy, precision, and recall. For instance, it might emerge that the classifier achieves an accuracy rate of 85%, implying it correctly predicts the sentiment of 85% of movie reviews in the testing set. Further insight into the classifier's performance can be obtained through a confusion matrix, visualizing its performance in finer detail.

Conclusion: This case study delves into employing the naïve Bayes algorithm for sentiment classification on movie reviews. The journey involves data preprocessing, classifier training, testing, and performance evaluation. Naïve Bayes, although simple, proves highly effective for sentiment classification and stands as a staple in NLP applications.

3

Smoothed Estimation and Language Modelling

When encountering words within our vocabulary that appear in an unfamiliar context during testing, certain smoothing techniques are employed to prevent language models from assigning a zero probability to these previously unseen combinations. This process, known as smoothing or discounting, involves real-locating a portion of probability mass from more frequent events to events that have not been observed before. This ensures that the model doesn't disregard unseen events entirely. Various smoothing methods exist, such as Laplace (add-one) smoothing, add-k smoothing, stupid backoff, and Kneser–Ney smoothing.

Smoothing techniques in the field of natural language processing (NLP) are aimed at resolving situations where the estimation of the likelihood or probability of a sequence of words is hindered by the presence of individual words or N-grams that have never appeared together before. These techniques address the challenge of making accurate probability estimates for sequences containing unseen combinations [12].

Language modelling plays a pivotal role in estimating the probability of word sequences. This practice finds applications in diverse areas including speech recognition, spam filtering, and more, forming the foundation of many advanced natural language processing models.

Language Modelling Methods

Two primary types of language modelling exist:

- **Statistical language modelling:** Statistical language modelling focuses on creating probabilistic models capable of predicting the subsequent word in a sequence, given the preceding words. This category encompasses examples like N-gram language modelling.

- **Neural language modelling:** Neural network methods have shown superiority over classical approaches both in standalone language models and when integrated into complex models for tasks like speech recognition and machine translation. Word embeddings are one way to execute neural language modelling.

3.1 N-gram Language Models: Understanding N-grams

N-gram language models: N-grams are contiguous sequences of N items derived from a given text or speech sample. These items can be letters, words, or base pairs, depending on the context. N-gram language models predict the probability of a given N-gram within any word sequence of a language. Effective N-gram models can forecast the subsequent word in a sentence, quantified by p(w|h), where h is the history.

For instance, unigrams like ("This", "article", "is", "on", "NLP") or bigrams like ("This article", "article is", "is on", "on NLP") exemplify N-grams. When estimating the probability P(w|h) of a word w given a history h, traditional methods involve relative frequency counts. However, this approach may fall short due to the creative nature of language, leading to the need for smoothing techniques [22].

N-gram language models hold a foundational role in NLP. They are employed to characterize the probability distribution of word or character sequences in text, enabling their application in various tasks like language modelling, machine translation, speech recognition, and text generation.

Here's an overview of how N-gram language models work:

1. **Corpus preparation:** The first step is to prepare a corpus of text data, which is a collection of documents or sentences. The corpus is used to guess the probabilities of different N-grams happening in the language.
2. **Tokenization:** The text is typically tokenized into words or characters. Each word or character becomes a token in the model. For example, the sentence "I love natural language processing" would be tokenized into individual words: ["I", "love", "natural", "language", "processing"].
3. **N-gram generation:** N-grams are generated by sliding a window of size N over the tokenized text. For example, for a 3-gram model, the sentence "I love natural language processing" would produce the following 3-grams: ["I love natural"], ["love natural language"], ["natural language processing"].
4. **Counting N-grams:** The next step is to count the occurrences of each N-gram in the corpus. This involves counting how many times each N-gram appears in the text data. These counts are used to estimate the probabilities of the N-grams.

5. **Probability estimation:** The counts of N-grams are secondhand to estimate the conditional probabilities of the next word or character assumed the previous N-1 words or characters. For example, to estimate the probability of a word W given the previous two words, P(W|W_1, W_2), the count of the 3-gram [W_1, W_2, W] is divided by the count of the 2-gram [W_1, W_2].

6. **Smoothing:** In practice, N-gram models often encounter unseen N-grams, i.e. N-grams that did not occur in the training corpus. Smoothing techniques such as add-k smoothing or backoff methods are employed to assign some probability mass to unseen N-grams, ensuring a more robust language model.

7. **Language modeling:** Once the N-gram probabilities are estimated, the perfect can be used for many NLP tasks. In language modeling, given a sequence of N − 1 words or characters, the model predicts the next word or character by selecting the one with the highest conditional probability.

N-gram language models are simple yet powerful tools for capturing the statistical properties of natural language. They provide a foundation for understanding the structure and patterns of manuscript data, and they form the basis for more advanced techniques in NLP.

3.2 Assessing Language Models: Evaluation Strategies

Once a language model is constructed, it becomes imperative to assess its functionality. Evaluating language models involves the preparation of three distinct datasets, following a pattern analogous to many other machine learning models:

1. **Training data**: This set is employed to train the model's parameters, enabling it to learn from the data.

2. **Development data**: Often referred to as the validation set, it aids in making choices between alternate models or refining hyperparameters. Hyperparameters could involve aspects like the maximum length of N in an N-gram model or the type of smoothing technique.

3. **Test data**: This set serves as the ultimate benchmark to measure the model's accuracy and report final results.

Language model evaluation seeks to determine the model's accuracy in representing language. Several metrics exist for this purpose, with likelihood and log likelihood being fundamental choices. Likelihood corresponds to the model's probability assignment to development or test data. Log likelihood is commonly preferred due to computational efficiency and mathematical convenience. It's customary to normalize log likelihood by the number of words in the corpus, making comparison feasible across corpora of varying lengths.

The most robust method for evaluating a language model is to embed it in an application and gauge its impact on performance. This approach, termed extrinsic evaluation, provides a real-world assessment of the model's effectiveness. For instance, in speech recognition, comparing transcriptions from two language models within the speech recognizer can establish which model yields superior accuracy.

However, full-scale end-to-end evaluation is often resource-intensive. Therefore, intrinsic evaluation metrics, which gauge model quality independently of applications, become crucial. For intrinsic evaluation, a test set is essential. The probabilities generated by an N-gram model stem from the training corpus. Thus, the quality of an N-gram model can be measured using a test set, representing unseen data.

Perplexity emerges as a common measure for language model accuracy. It denotes the exponent of the average negative log likelihood per word. In a more intuitive sense, perplexity gauges the model's confusion level in decision-making. It asks, "If we randomly selected words from the probability distribution produced by the language model at each step, how many words would be required on average to select the correct one?" Perplexity is often used in research papers due to its larger values, which facilitate easy differentiation between models.

In essence, evaluating language models encompasses a range of methods, from application-driven extrinsic evaluation to intrinsic metrics like perplexity. Each approach contributes to comprehending a model's performance from diverse perspectives.

Evaluating language models in natural language processing (NLP) is crucial to assess their performance and determine their effectiveness in various tasks. Here are some common evaluation metrics and techniques used for language models:

1. **Perplexity:** Perplexity serves as a prevalent metric for assessing the effectiveness of language models. It quantifies how well a language model predicts a given text. A lower perplexity score signifies superior performance. Perplexity is determined by calculating the inverse probability of the test set and normalizing it by the number of words. This can be mathematically expressed as: perplexity $= \exp(-(1/N) * \log P(w\_1,w\_2,...,w\_N))$, where N represents the word count in the test set and $P(w\_1,w\_2,...,w\_N)$ corresponds to the probability assigned to the test set by the language model.

2. **Word error rate (WER):** WER is a widely used evaluation metric, especially in speech recognition tasks. It gauges the percentage of words in the model's output that differ from the reference transcription. Lower WER values indicate superior model performance.

3. **BLEU (bilingual evaluation understudy):** In the domain of machine translation, BLEU serves as a commonly adopted metric for evaluating translated text quality. BLEU assesses the alignment of N-grams (often up to 4-grams) in the generated translation against a set of reference translations. A higher BLEU score signifies better translation quality.

4. **ROUGE (recall-oriented understudy for gisting evaluation**): ROUGE comprises a suite of metrics predominantly utilized in text summarization tasks. It quantifies the overlap between the generated summary and reference summaries, employing N-gram matching and other similarity measures.

5. **F1 score:** The F1 score finds utility in evaluating models across various tasks such as text classification, named entity recognition, and sentiment analysis. This score amalgamates precision and recall to provide a unified assessment measure. Precision assesses the model's ability to correctly identify positive instances, while recall evaluates the model's capability to locate all positive instances. The F1 score is the harmonic mean of precision and recall, effectively encapsulating both aspects of model performance.

6. **Human evaluation:** In some cases, human evaluation is conducted to assess the quality of language models. Human evaluators may assess the fluency, correctness, coherence, and overall quality of the generated text. This evaluation approach can provide valuable insights but can be resource intensive.

It's important to consider the specific task and requirements when selecting appropriate evaluation metrics. Evaluating language models often involves a combination of objective metrics and qualitative assessments to gain a comprehensive understanding of their performance and limitations.

3.3 Challenges in Language Modelling

The language modelling problem within the realm of natural language processing (NLP) revolves around the task of predicting the next word or sequence of words in a given context. Language models, rooted in statistical methodologies, undergo training on extensive text datasets to glean patterns, relationships, and the likelihood of word sequences.

The core objective of language modelling is to encapsulate the intricate structure and semantics of language, empowering the model to generate coherent and contextually relevant text. These language models play a pivotal role as fundamental components across a spectrum of NLP applications, spanning machine translation, speech recognition, text generation, and sentiment analysis.

Diverse approaches exist for constructing language models, with one prominent method revolving around N-grams. N-grams denote consecutive sequences of N words within a text, wherein bigrams comprise two consecutive words and trigrams encompass three. N-gram language models estimate the likelihood of the subsequent word based on the prior N − 1 words by tallying the occurrences of N-grams within a training corpus.

Another widespread approach involves neural networks, particularly recurrent neural networks (RNNs) and more advanced iterations like long short-term memory (LSTM) networks and transformer models. These neural architectures are trained to comprehend word relationships and capture contextual dependencies across lengthy sequences of text.

Language models typically undergo training on expansive datasets like Wikipedia articles, books, or web text, in a bid to fathom the statistical properties of language. The training process revolves around refining the model's parameters to minimize discrepancies between predicted and actual word sequences within the training data. Common techniques encompass maximum likelihood estimation or adaptations like masked language modelling, as observed in transformer models.

Once trained, language models find multifaceted utility. They can predict upcoming words based on context, generate text from scratch, complete partial sentences, and assess sentence likelihood. Furthermore, these models can be fine-tuned for specific tasks or domains to enhance their performance in specialized applications.

In recent times, the large-scale pretraining and fine-tuning of transformer-based language models, exemplified by OpenAI's GPT series, have showcased exceptional accomplishments across diverse NLP tasks. These models have made notable strides in realms such as machine translation, question answering, text summarization, and even creative writing, underscoring their prowess in natural language comprehension and generation.

These neural network-based language models can capture longer-term dependencies and context in text by considering the entire input sequence. They use techniques such as sequence-to-sequence modeling, attention mechanisms, and self-attention to learn and generate coherent and contextually appropriate text. Models like OpenAI's GPT (generative pre-trained transformer) have achieved impressive results in various language tasks by leveraging large-scale pre-training on vast amounts of text data.

One challenge in language modeling is handling out-of-vocabulary (OOV) words or rare word occurrences. This requires techniques such as sub-word tokenization or using character-level models to handle unseen words effectively.

Overall, language modeling is a crucial task in NLP that enables an extensive variety of applications by providing models with the ability to generate, understand, and manipulate natural language text.

3.3.1 Dealing with generalization and zero frequency

In the context of language modeling, generalization refers to the ability of a language model to accurately predict and generate meaningful text in situations that it has not been explicitly trained on. Generalization is crucial for language models to handle unseen or out-of-distribution data and to perform well on diverse language tasks.

Language models are trained on huge amounts of text data, typically from a specific domain or a mixture of domains. However, it is not possible to include all possible sentences and word combinations in the training data. Therefore, language models need to generalize well by capturing the underlying patterns, structures, and semantics of the language. This allows them to generate coherent and contextually appropriate text even for inputs that are not explicitly seen during training.

Generalization in language modeling can be challenging due to several reasons. One common issue is the presence of rare or infrequent words, also known as the "long tail" problem. If a language model encounters a rare word during generation that it has not seen frequently during training, it may struggle to generate the correct word or might produce incorrect or nonsensical output. Techniques such as sub-word tokenization or character-level modeling can help mitigate this problem by representing words in smaller units that are more likely to be seen during training.

Another aspect related to generalization is handling syntactic and semantic variations. Language models need to understand the underlying grammatical structures, word order, and semantic relationships in order to generate coherent text. Generalizing across different sentence structures, word placements, and semantic variations is essential for producing meaningful and contextually appropriate responses.

On the other hand, "zeros" in the language modeling problem refer to the occurrence of unseen or unknown words during text generation. These could be words that are not present in the training data or are rare and infrequent. Dealing with zeros is a challenge because language models need to handle such cases gracefully without breaking the flow of generated text.

To address the zero problem, language models often rely on statistical techniques like smoothing or backoff methods. These methods assign a small probability mass to unseen words or N-grams, allowing the model to generate plausible text even when encountering unknown words. Additionally, techniques like sub-word tokenization, as mentioned earlier, can help handle zeros by breaking down words into smaller units that are more likely to be seen during training.

In summary, generalization is a crucial aspect of language modeling that enables models to generate meaningful and coherent text in various scenarios. Dealing with zeros or unseen words requires techniques like sub-word tokenization, statistical smoothing, and handling syntactic and semantic variations to ensure the model's robustness and effectiveness in generating text.

For N-grams that have occurred a sufficient number of times, we can typically estimate their probabilities with a reasonable level of accuracy. However, due to the inherent limitations of any corpus, there will inevitably be valid English word sequences missing from it. Consequently, numerous instances of what might be perceived as "zero probability N-grams" should actually possess non-zero probabilities.

Let's take into consideration the occurrences of words following the bigram "denied the" in the WSJ Treebank3 corpus, along with their respective counts:

- Denied the allegations: 5
- Denied the speculation: 2
- Denied the rumors: 1
- Denied the report: 1.

However, let's imagine our test set contains phrases like:

- Denied the offer
- Denied the loan.

In this scenario, our language model could mistakenly deduce that P(offer denied the) is equal to 0. This occurrence of zero probabilities in the training set but not in the test set poses two distinct challenges. Firstly, this leads to an underestimation of the likelihood of various potential words, adversely affecting the performance of any applications applied to the data. Secondly, when the probability of any word in the test set becomes 0, the entire probability of the test set becomes 0. As perplexity relies on the inverse probability of the test set, the presence of words with zero probability renders perplexity calculations impossible due to division by zero.

3.3.2 Addressing unknown words

In the previous section, we explored the issue of words with zero bigram probabilities. However, what about words that are completely novel to us? In certain language tasks, the presence of such words might be ruled out due to the knowledge of all potential words that could arise.

In closed vocabulary systems, the test set solely comprises words from a predetermined lexicon, thereby obviating the presence of unknown words. This is particularly applicable in domains like speech recognition or machine translation, where the model's vocabulary is constrained by a fixed dictionary or phrase table.

In contrast, certain situations necessitate dealing with words that have not been previously encountered—referred to as unknown words or out-of-vocabulary (OOV) words. The fraction of OOV words in the test set is known as the OOV rate. In open vocabulary systems, the modelling of these potential unknown words is achieved by introducing a pseudo-word called "<UNK>."

Two common strategies for training the probabilities of the unknown word model ("<UNK>") are prevalent. The first approach involves reverting to a closed vocabulary setup:

1. Preselect a fixed vocabulary (word list).
2. During training, convert any word not present in this predefined vocabulary (OOV word) into the <UNK> token through text normalization.
3. Estimate the probabilities for <UNK> based on its counts, akin to any other regular word in the training set.

The second alternative, applicable when a predefined vocabulary isn't available, entails implicitly creating such a vocabulary by replacing words in the training data with <UNK> based on their frequency [13].

Handling unknown words (also known as out-of-vocabulary or OOV words) is a significant challenge in the language modeling problem. Unidentified words are words that are not present in the vocabulary or training data of a language model. These can be proper nouns, misspellings, rare words, or words from a different language.

Dealing with unknown words is crucial because encountering them during text generation or prediction can lead to incorrect or nonsensical outputs. Here are a few common approaches to handle unknown words:

1. **Out-of-vocabulary token:** One common technique is to introduce a special token, often denoted as <UNK>, to represent unknown words. During training, if a word is not present in the vocabulary, it is replaced with the <UNK> token. This allows the model to learn a representation for unknown words. During generation or prediction, when the model encounters an unknown word, it can use the <UNK> token to indicate its presence.

2. **Sub-word tokenization:** Another approach is to use sub-word tokenization methods such as byte-pair encoding (BPE) or WordPiece. These methods break down words into smaller sub-word units, which are then treated as separate tokens. This helps in handling unknown words because even if a word is unseen during training, its sub-word units might be present in the vocabulary. This approach is particularly effective for handling rare or morphologically rich languages.

3. **Morphological analysis:** In some cases, unknown words can be analyzed morphologically to infer their meaning or possible word forms. Morphological analyzers or stemmers can be employed to break down unknown words into their root forms or morphemes. This permits the prototypical to make better forecasts based on the morphological structure of the word.

4. **External resources:** Language models can also benefit from external resources like dictionaries, thesauri, or pre-trained word embeddings. These resources can be used to map unknown words to similar or related words that are present in the vocabulary. This can provide context and meaning to the unknown word during generation or prediction.

5. **Contextual clues:** Language models can utilize contextual clues from the surrounding words to infer the meaning or likely candidates for unknown words. By considering the context and syntactic structure of the sentence, the model can make more informed predictions for unknown words.

Handling unknown words in language modeling is an vigorous area of study, and dissimilar approaches can be combined or adapted based on the specific task and domain. The goal is to provide the model with enough information to generate coherent and contextually appropriate text, even when faced with words that it has not encountered during training.

4

Semantic Analysis and Discourse Processing

Semantic analysis is a crucial subfield within natural language processing (NLP) that aims to unravel the meaning inherent in human language. Although understanding natural language might seem intuitive to humans, the intricacies and subjectivity embedded in linguistic expressions make it a complex challenge for machines to decipher. Semantic analysis in NLP seeks to decipher the significance of provided text while factoring in context, logical sentence structuring, and grammatical roles.

Discourse processing represents a comprehensive suite of natural language processing (NLP) tasks designed to unveil linguistic structures within texts across various levels, thereby lending support to a multitude of downstream applications [17].

In the realm of artificial intelligence, the most intricate endeavor lies in enabling computers to process natural language. Put differently, natural language processing emerges as the most formidable challenge within the scope of artificial intelligence. When delving into the principal challenges within NLP, discourse processing takes center stage—a pursuit cantered around constructing theories and models that elucidate how utterances coalesce to form coherent discourse. In actuality, language predominantly comprises cohesive, structured, and interconnected collections of sentences, as opposed to isolated and disjointed statements often portrayed in movies. These interconnected collections of sentences are commonly referred to as discourse.

Semantic analysis and discourse processing hold profound significance as vital domains within the sphere of NLP, contributing to the comprehension of linguistic meaning and the intricate architecture of human language.

Semantic analysis, also known as semantic understanding or semantic parsing, focuses on extracting the meaning from a given text or sentence. It involves mapping the words and phrases in a sentence to their corresponding semantic representations or concepts. The goal is to capture the underlying meaning of the text rather than just its surface form.

There are several techniques and approaches used in semantic analysis, including:

1. **Named entity recognition (NER):** NER involves the identification and categorization of named entities like individuals, organizations, locations, dates, etc. This process aids in recognizing significant entities mentioned within the text.
2. **Word sense disambiguation (WSD):** WSD tackles the challenge of determining the correct meaning of ambiguous words based on the context they are used in. For instance, disambiguating the word "bank" to either refer to a financial institution or the side of a river.
3. **Semantic role labelling (SRL):** SRL entails assigning semantic roles to words or phrases present in a sentence, such as identifying the subject, object, or the action being carried out. This aids in comprehending the interrelations between various components of the sentence.
4. **Sentiment analysis:** Sentiment analysis involves gauging the emotional sentiment or tone conveyed within a text—whether it is positive, negative, or neutral. This analytical approach finds application in areas such as monitoring social media, analyzing customer feedback, and extracting opinions.

Discourse processing, on the other hand, deals with the analysis of how sentences and utterances are connected and organized to form coherent and meaningful texts or conversations. It involves understanding the discourse structure, coherence relations, and discourse markers that guide the flow of information and convey the speaker's intention [17].

Some key tasks in discourse processing include:

1. **Discourse parsing:** Analyzing the structure and organization of a discourse, such as identifying discourse segments, discourse relations, and discourse connectives.
2. **Coreference resolution:** Resolving references to entities or events across multiple sentences or utterances. This helps in understanding how pronouns, definite noun phrases, or other referring expressions relate to their antecedents.
3. **Text coherence and cohesion:** Assessing the overall coherence and cohesion of a text by examining the relationships between sentences or discourse units. This involves detecting and resolving lexical, grammatical, and rhetorical devices that contribute to text coherence.
4. **Discourse generation:** Generating coherent and contextually appropriate responses or texts in natural language. This is particularly relevant in dialogue systems and conversational agents.

Both semantic analysis and discourse processing are essential for many NLP claims, counting question answering, information retrieval, machine translation, dialogue systems, and text summarization. These techniques help in extracting meaningful information, understanding user intent, and generating coherent and contextually relevant responses in natural language.

4.1 Semantic Analysis: Representing Meaning

Semantic analysis involves deriving meaning from text, enabling computers to interpret and comprehend sentences, paragraphs, or entire documents. This is achieved through the examination of their grammatical composition and the identification of connections between individual words within a specific context. It encompasses the process of extracting meaningful insights, including context, emotions, and sentiments, from unstructured data in natural language.

Semantic analysis in natural language processing (NLP) involves the task of representing the meaning of text in a structured and formal manner. The goal is to capture the underlying semantics or semantic relationships between words, phrases, and sentences. There are various approaches to meaning representation in NLP, and here are a few common ones:

1. **Lexical semantics:** Lexical semantics focuses on representing the meanings of individual words or lexical items. One popular approach is the use of semantic networks or ontologies, such as WordNet. WordNet organizes words into synsets (sets of synonymous words) and provides relationships between them, such as hypernymy (is-a relationship) and hyponymy (part-of relationship).

2. **Distributional semantics:** Distributional semantics is grounded on the idea that words with similar distributions in the text tend to have similar meanings. It represents word meaning through distributional word vectors, often obtained through methods like word2vec or GloVe. These word vectors capture the co-occurrence patterns of words in large text corpora.

3. **Logical formalisms:** Logical formalisms, such as first-order logic or higher-order logic, provide a formal language for representing the meaning of sentences. They use logical operators, quantifiers, and variables to express relationships and constraints within a sentence. Semantic parsing techniques convert natural language sentences into logical forms for further processing and reasoning.

4. **Frame semantics:** Frame semantics represents meaning in terms of conceptual frames, which are cognitive structures that capture knowledge about specific scenarios or situations. Frames consist of semantic roles, which describe the participants and their roles in an event, and frame elements, which represent the attributes and characteristics associated with the event.

5. **Dependency-based representations:** Dependency-based representations model the syntactic structure of sentences using dependency relationships between words. Dependency parsing algorithms assign grammatical relationships, such as subject, object, or modifier, to each word in a sentence. These dependencies can be leveraged to capture semantic relationships as well.

It's important to note that meaning representation in NLP is an ongoing research area, and different approaches have their strengths and limitations. Often, a combination of these techniques is used in practical systems to capture various aspects of meaning. The choice of meaning representation depends on the specific task at hand and the available resources.

4.2 Exploring Lexical Semantics

This phase marks the initial step in semantic analysis, focusing on comprehending the significance of individual words. It encompasses the study of words, sub-words, affixes (sub-units), compound words, and phrases. Collectively, these elements are referred to as lexical items.

To put it simply, lexical semantics delves into the associations among lexical items, the meaning of sentences, and the syntax of those sentences. The process of lexical semantics involves the following key steps:

- Categorizing lexical items.
- Dissecting the components of lexical items.
- Analyzing both distinctions and parallels among various lexical-semantic structures.

Say for example: forward.

Let us take two sentences.

"Forward into the ocean."

"She was leaning forward."

We can separate forward in both these cases.

"Forward" or "forward" operates in two different contexts relating to other words.

Lexical semantics is a subfield of natural language processing (NLP) that focuses on the sense of individual words or lexical items and their relationships.

It aims to represent the meanings of words and how they interact with each other in a language [18].

Here are some key aspects of lexical semantics in NLP:

1. **Word sense disambiguation (WSD):** In natural language, numerous words possess multiple meanings or senses. Word sense disambiguation refers to the process of identifying the accurate sense of a word within a specific context. This task entails associating a word with the most fitting sense from a predefined inventory of senses, often based on resources like WordNet. WSD plays a pivotal role in comprehending the intended significance of words within a sentence and finds utility in a range of NLP applications, including machine translation, information retrieval, and question answering.

2. **Lexical resources:** Lexical resources play a significant role in lexical semantics. These resources provide structured information about words, including their meanings, senses, relationships, and properties. WordNet is one of the most extensively used lexical resources. It organizes words into synsets (sets of synonymous words) and provides information about their relationships, such as hypernymy (is-a relationship), hyponymy (part-of relationship), and meronymy (part-whole relationship). Other resources like FrameNet, ConceptNet, and VerbNet offer additional lexical information for specific domains or semantic frameworks.

3. **Semantic similarity:** Lexical semantics also deals with measuring the semantic similarity between words or phrases. It aims to quantify the relatedness or similarity in meaning between different words. Various techniques are used for computing semantic similarity, including comparing word vectors based on distributional semantics, using knowledge-based approaches that leverage lexical resources, or combining multiple sources of information. Semantic similarity measures are useful in tasks like information retrieval, recommendation systems, and automatic summarization.

4. **Lexical relations:** Lexical semantics explores the relationships between words. These relationships provide insights into the semantic structure of a language. Some common lexical relations include synonymity (words with similar meanings), antonymy (words with contradictory senses), meronymy (part-whole relationships), and hypernymy/hyponymy (superordinate and subordinate relationships). Identifying and understanding these relationships helps in building more accurate models for various NLP tasks.

5. **Lexical acquisition:** Lexical semantics is also concerned with the acquisition of lexical knowledge. This involves automatically extracting semantic information from large corpora, aligning words with their appropriate senses, and building or expanding lexical resources. Lexical acquisition techniques contribute to improving the coverage and accuracy of lexical semantics in NLP systems.

Lexical semantics plays a vital part in various NLP applications, including information retrieval, machine translation, question answering, sentiment analysis, and text generation. By capturing the meanings and relationships of words, lexical semantics enables more accurate and nuanced language understanding and generation by NLP models.

4.3 Navigating Ambiguity

Ambiguity, a concept commonly encountered in natural language processing, pertains to the capacity of a linguistic expression to possess multiple interpretations. Put simply, ambiguity signifies the potential to be comprehended in more than one manner. Natural language is inherently rich with ambiguity, often allowing for diverse interpretations of the same expression. Ambiguity is a common challenge in natural language processing (NLP) due to the inherent complexity and richness of human language. It refers to situations where a word, phrase, or sentence can have multiple possible interpretations or meanings. Ambiguity poses difficulties in understanding and processing language accurately, as the intended meaning may be uncertain. Here are a few types of ambiguity that arise in NLP:

1. **Lexical ambiguity:** Lexical ambiguity emerges when a single word possesses multiple meanings. For instance, the term "bank" could denote either a financial establishment or the shoreline of a water body. To address lexical ambiguity, one must analyze the contextual surroundings to ascertain the intended signification.

2. **Syntactic ambiguity**: Syntactic ambiguity surfaces when a sentence can be structurally parsed in various ways, resulting in distinct potential interpretations. This can occur due to the presence of ambiguous phrases, attachments, or structural ambiguities. For instance, in the sentence "Visiting relatives can be tiresome," it is unclear whether "visiting" modifies "relatives" or serves as the subject of the sentence.

3. **Semantic ambiguity:** Semantic ambiguity refers to situations where a sentence or phrase can be interpreted in multiple ways due to its underlying meaning. It involves understanding the intended sense or concept rather than the surface form. For example, the sentence "He saw her duck" could mean that he observed her lowering her head or that he observed a duck belonging to her.

4. **Pragmatic ambiguity:** Pragmatic ambiguity arises when the meaning of a statement depends on the context, speaker's intention, or shared background knowledge. It involves considering factors beyond the words themselves, such as implied meaning, sarcasm, or indirect speech acts. Resolving pragmatic ambiguity often requires incorporating contextual and situational cues.

Dealing with ambiguity is a significant challenge in NLP. To address it, various techniques and strategies are employed, including:

- **Contextual information:** Leveraging contextual information, such as surrounding words or sentences, to disambiguate the intended meaning.
- **Statistical methods:** Utilizing statistical models that learn from large corpora to capture the most likely interpretations based on frequency and co-occurrence patterns.
- **Machine learning:** Employing machine learning algorithms to train models on labeled data, allowing them to make more accurate predictions and disambiguate ambiguous language.
- **Knowledge resources:** Utilizing lexical resources like WordNet or domain-specific ontologies to provide additional information about word senses and relationships.
- **Discourse analysis:** Considering the broader discourse or conversation to infer the intended meaning based on previous or subsequent statements.

Addressing ambiguity in NLP is an ongoing research area, and advancements in techniques like deep learning, contextual embeddings, and pre-training models have shown promising results in improving disambiguation accuracy. However, complete disambiguation in all cases remains a challenging task, and the interpretation of ambiguous language can still vary depending on the specific context and the knowledge available to the NLP system.

4.4 Resolving Word Sense Ambiguity

Word sense disambiguation (WSD), a fundamental challenge in natural language processing (NLP), involves determining the appropriate meaning of a word based on its usage within a specific context. Within NLP, grappling with the intricacies of lexical ambiguity, whether they be syntactic or semantic, is among the primary hurdles. While part-of-speech (POS) taggers can adeptly handle syntactic ambiguity by accurately assigning parts of speech, the more intricate task of untangling semantic ambiguity is termed word sense disambiguation.

To illustrate, consider the word "bass" and its dual meanings:

- "I can hear the bass sound."
- "He likes to eat grilled bass."

In the above instances, the word "bass" distinctly signifies different concepts. In the first sentence, it denotes a musical frequency, while in the second, it refers to a type of fish. Through effective WSD, the respective meanings can be correctly attributed to the sentences:

- "I can hear bass/frequency sound."
- "He likes to eat grilled bass/fish."

Consequently, WSD plays a pivotal role in enabling accurate language understanding and interpretation within various NLP applications.

Word sense disambiguation (WSD) is a crucial mission in natural language processing (NLP) that aims to determine the correct sense of a word in a given context. It addresses the challenge of lexical ambiguity, where a word can have numerous meanings or senses dependent on the context in which it is used. The goal of WSD is to identify the intended sense of the word to enable accurate language understanding and processing. Here are key aspects of word sense disambiguation:

1. **Sense inventory:** WSD relies on a sense inventory, which is a predefined set of senses or meanings associated with each word. Lexical resources like WordNet provide sense inventories that organize words into synsets, where each synset represents a specific sense of a word. For instance, the word "bank" in WordNet has different synsets representing the financial institution sense and the river bank sense.

2. **Contextual information:** WSD leverages the surrounding context of a word to disambiguate its meaning. The context includes neighboring words, phrases, syntactic structures, and some-times broader discourse. By considering the words and their relationships within the context, WSD algorithms attempt to identify the sense that best fits the given context.

3. **Supervised and unsupervised approaches:** WSD can be approached through supervised or unsupervised learning methods. In supervised approaches, annotated training data is used, where each word occurrence is labeled with the corresponding sense. Machine learning proce-dures, such as decision trees, support vector machines, or neural networks, are then trained on this data to learn the mapping between word contexts and senses. Unsupervised approaches, on the other hand, do not require labeled data and typically rely on statistical or clustering techniques to identify patterns in word usage and group similar contexts together.

4. **Knowledge-based methods:** Knowledge-based WSD methods leverage lexical resources and linguistic knowledge to disambiguate word senses. These methods utilize the sense inven-tory provided by resources like WordNet and employ various techniques such as graph-based algorithms, knowledge-based reasoning, or similarity measures to regulate the most proper sense for a given word in context.

5. **Disambiguation techniques:** Different disambiguation techniques are used in WSD, including:

    - **Lesk algorithm:** The Lesk algorithm compares the glosses (definitions) of dif-ferent senses of a word with the surrounding context to find the most related sense.
    - **Supervised classification:** This approach involves training machine learning models using labeled data to classify word instances into their correct senses based on contextual features.

- **Word embeddings:** Word embeddings, such as word2vec or GloVe, can be utilized to represent words as dense vectors capturing their semantic properties. WSD models can exploit these embeddings to estimate the similarity between word contexts and possible senses.

WSD has applications in various NLP responsibilities such as machine translation, information retrieval, question answering, and text summarization. By disambiguating word senses, NLP systems can improve their accuracy and understanding of language, leading to more reliable and precise language processing outcomes. However, WSD remains a challenging task, particularly in cases of subtle contextual differences or when senses are closely related. Ongoing research focuses on combining multiple approaches, leveraging large-scale language models, and exploring contextualized word representations to enhance WSD performance.

4.5 Discourse Processing: Cohesion in Text

In natural language processing (NLP), discourse processing involves analyzing the structure, coherence, and cohesion of texts or conversations. Cohesion, specifically, refers to the ways in which various linguistic elements within a discourse are connected to create a coherent and unified piece of text. It involves the use of explicit and implicit devices to establish relationships between sentences, paragraphs, or utterances. Here are some key aspects of cohesion in discourse processing:

1. **Reference:** Reference involves using words or expressions to refer back to previously mentioned entities or concepts. Pronouns, definite noun phrases, and demonstratives are common examples of referring expressions. Establishing clear referential links contributes to the cohesion of a text and avoids ambiguity.
   Example: "John bought a book. He enjoys reading it every evening."
2. **Ellipsis:** Ellipsis is the error of words or phrases that can be inferred from the framework. It helps avoid repetition and maintains textual cohesion. Elliptical constructions often occur when a previously mentioned element is repeated or redundant.
   Example: "Jane likes coffee, and Peter does too." (omitting "likes coffee").
3. **Conjunctions and connectives:** Conjunctions and connectives are words or phrases that explicitly indicate relationships between sentences or discourse units. They contribute to the coherence of a text by indicating logical connections, contrasts, cause-effect relationships, or temporal sequences.
   Example: "I went to the store, and I bought some groceries." (using the conjunction "and" to show addition).

4. **Lexical cohesion:** Lexical cohesion involves the use of related or synonymous words or expressions to establish connections across sentences. Repetition, synonyms, antonyms, and hyponyms can all contribute to lexical cohesion.
   Example: "The dog barked loudly. It made a lot of noise." (using synonyms "barked" and "made a lot of noise").

5. **Parallelism:** Parallelism refers to the repetition of grammatical structures, phrases, or patterns across sentences or discourse units. It enhances the flow and coherence of a text by creating a sense of symmetry or balance.
   Example: "She likes hiking, swimming, and cycling." (using parallel gerunds).

6. **Coherence markers:** Coherence markers, such as discourse markers or transitional phrases, explicitly signal the organization and flow of information within a discourse. They help guide the reader or listener and indicate relationships between ideas.
   Example: "Firstly, let's discuss the problem. Secondly, we can propose some solutions."

Cohesion plays a crucial role in discourse understanding and generation. By identifying and leveraging cohesive devices, NLP systems can improve the coherence and understandability of generated texts, dialogue systems, or summarization outputs. Discourse parsing and analysis techniques are employed to identify and model cohesive relationships, ensuring that the information flows smoothly and coherently within a discourse.

Cohesion pertains to the interconnectedness of ideas within a text or sentence, encompassing both grammatical and lexical relationships that provide the framework for conveying meaning.

Two primary categories of cohesion exist:

- **Grammatical cohesion:** Grounded in structural aspects.
- **Lexical cohesion:** Anchored in lexical content and contextual understanding.

Various methods contribute to the establishment of a cohesive text. In their work "Cohesion in English," M A K Halliday and Ruqaiya Hasan identify five broad groups of cohesive devices that contribute to textual coherence: reference, ellipsis, substitution, lexical cohesion, and conjunction. These mechanisms collectively foster a seamless flow of ideas, ensuring the coherence and intelligibility of the text.

4.5.1 Referencing

Referential devices play a crucial role in creating cohesion within text. Two forms of referencing contribute to this cohesion:

- **Anaphoric reference** occurs when a writer refers back to a previously mentioned entity to prevent redundancy. Examples include substituting "the taxi driver" with the pronoun "he" or "two girls" with "they." Formulaic sequences like "as stated previously" also fall under this category.
- **Cataphoric reference**, in contrast to anaphora, involves a reference forward in the discourse. It introduces an entity abstractly before its identification. For instance: "Here he comes, our award-winning host...it's John Doe!" Cataphoric references also manifest in written text. There is another form of referencing that doesn't foster cohesion:
- **Exophoric reference** pertains to generics or abstract concepts without explicit identification. Unlike anaphora and cataphora, which identify entities (endophora), exophoric reference uses generic terms like "everything." The prefix "exo" signifies "outside," and entities referred to in this manner remain unidentified by the writer. Halliday and Hasan view exophoric reference as non-cohesive since it doesn't establish a connection between elements in the text.
- **Homophobic reference** is a generic phrase whose specific meaning is derived from its contextual knowledge. For instance, the interpretation of "the Queen" depends on the context of its use.

4.6 Achieving Reference Resolution

Interpreting sentences within discourse involves determining the entities or individuals being referred to, which relies on reference resolution. Reference refers to linguistic expressions denoting entities, such as "Ram," "His," or "He." Reference resolution, in turn, identifies the entities referred to by these linguistic expressions.

4.6.1 Terminology in reference resolution

The following terms are used in reference resolution:

- **Referring expression:** A natural language expression used for reference, like the example passage.
- **Referent:** The entity being referred to, such as "Ram" in the example.
- **Corefer:** When two expressions refer to the same entity, they are coreferential (e.g., "Ram" and "he").
- **Antecedent:** A term that allows the use of another term, like "Ram" being the antecedent of "he."
- **Anaphora and anaphoric:** Referring to an entity previously introduced in the discourse. The referring expression is anaphoric.
- **Discourse model:** A model representing referred entities and their relationships in the discourse.

4.6.2 Types of referring expressions

Several types of referring expressions exist:

- **Indefinite noun phrases:** Referring to new entities in the discourse context, e.g., "some food."
- **Definite noun phrases:** Referring to known entities, e.g., "The Times of India."
- **Pronouns:** Definite references, e.g., "he" in "Ram laughed as loud as he could."
- **Demonstratives:** Demonstrative pronouns like "this" and "that."
- **Names:** Simplest referring expressions, e.g., "Ram."

4.6.3 Reference resolution tasks

Two key reference resolution tasks include:

1. **Coreference resolution:** Identifying referring expressions that refer to the same entity, forming coreference chains, e.g., "He," "Chief Manager," and "His." Constraints: English's challenge is pronoun "it," which has multiple uses and references.
2. **Pronominal anaphora resolution:** Identifying the antecedent for a single pronoun, e.g., resolving "his" to "Ram."

Reference resolution is a key task in natural language processing (NLP) that involves identifying and connecting referring expressions (e.g., pronouns, definite noun phrases) to the entities or concepts they refer to in a given context. It aims to resolve the ambiguity and establish the correct referents for these expressions, enabling accurate understanding and interpretation of language. Here are some important aspects of reference resolution in NLP:

1. **Pronoun resolution:** Pronouns such as "he," "she," "it," and "they" are commonly used in language to refer back to previously mentioned entities. Pronoun resolution involves determining the antecedent (the noun or noun phrase the pronoun refers to) based on the surrounding context. Resolving pronouns correctly is essential for maintaining coherence and understanding in a discourse.
   Example: "John saw Mary. He greeted her." In this case, the pronouns "He" and "her" refer to "John" and "Mary," respectively.
2. **Definite noun phrase resolution:** Definite noun phrases, such as "the car" or "this book," refer to specific entities within a discourse. Resolving definite noun phrases involves identifying the correct referents based on context and shared knowledge.
   Example: "I saw the car. It was parked near the house." Here, the definite noun phrase "the car" is resolved to the car that was previously mentioned.

3. **Coreference resolution:** Coreference resolution is the task of linking multiple mentioning words within a discourse to the same entity. It involves identifying when different expressions refer to the same person, object, or concept. Coreference resolution plays a crucial role in understanding the relationships between entities and establishing coherence in a text.
   Example: "John called his mother. He wanted to wish her a happy birthday." In this instance, coreference resolution connects the pronouns "his" and "he" to "John" and the pronoun "her" to "his mother."

4. **Anaphora resolution:** Anaphora resolution deals with resolving anaphoric expressions, which refer back to something mentioned earlier in the discourse. Anaphoric expressions can be pronouns, definite noun phrases, or other referring expressions [19].
   Example: "John bought a car. It is red." In this case, the anaphoric expression "It" refers back to the car mentioned earlier in the discourse.

Reference resolution is a stimulating task in NLP, as it requires considering the surrounding context, world knowledge, and linguistic cues to infer the correct referents. Various techniques are used for reference resolution, including rule-based approaches, machine learning models, and deep learning methods. These methods leverage syntactic and semantic features, discourse context, and statistical patterns to resolve references accurately. Reference resolution is critical in many NLP claims, such as question answering, data extraction, dialogue systems, and text summarization. By correctly resolving references, NLP systems can enhance their understanding of text, generate more coherent responses, and improve the overall accuracy and quality of language processing outcomes.

4.7 Establishing Discourse Coherence and Structure

Coherence and discourse structure share intricate connections that hold significant importance, especially when assessing the output quality of natural language generation systems. However, defining coherence in text raises a critical question: What exactly constitutes a coherent text? For instance, if we were to gather a sentence from every page of a newspaper, would this assortment qualify as a discourse? Clearly not, as these sentences lack the essential attribute of coherence. A truly coherent discourse should possess the following characteristics:

1. Coherence relations between utterances: The coherence of a discourse hinges on establishing meaningful connections between its individual utterances. This aspect is referred to as coherence relation. To exemplify, these connections should be supported by explanatory elements that justify their existence.

1. **Relationship among entities:** Another factor that contributes to discourse coherence is the existence of relationships between entities. This form of coherence is termed entity-based coherence. It implies that a discourse should exhibit a discernible connection or association among the entities mentioned.

2. **Discourse structure:** An inherent query pertaining to discourse revolves around its structural composition. The answer to this question relies on how the discourse has been segmented. Discourse segmentation refers to determining the structural arrangements within larger discourse. While discourse segmentation can be challenging to implement, it holds immense significance for applications like information retrieval, text summarization, and information extraction [21].

Discourse coherence and structure play a vital role in natural language processing (NLP) by providing organization and coherence to a text or conversation. They focus on the arrangement and flow of information, ensuring that the different parts of a discourse are connected and form a coherent and meaningful whole. Here are some key aspects of discourse coherence and structure in NLP:

1. **Discourse coherence:** Discourse coherence refers to the overall clarity and logical connection of ideas within a discourse. It involves maintaining a smooth and coherent flow of information from one sentence or utterance to the next. Coherence ensures that the information presented in a text or conversation is understandable and meaningful to the reader or listener.

2. **Coherence relations:** Coherence relations establish the logical or semantic connections between sentences or utterances in a discourse. These relations help in understanding the relationships between ideas and provide a structure to the discourse. Examples of coherence relations include cause–effect, temporal order, comparison, contrast, and elaboration. Recognizing and capturing these coherence relations aids in understanding the intended meaning and organizing the discourse.

3. **Discourse markers:** Discourse markers are words or phrases that signal the relationships between sentences or utterances and guide the flow of information in a discourse. They provide explicit cues about the coherence relations present in the discourse. Examples of discourse markers include "however," "moreover," "on the other hand," and "for example." Understanding and using discourse markers is crucial for building coherent and well-structured language models.

4. **Textual cohesion:** Textual cohesion focuses on the linguistic and semantic connections between different parts of a discourse. It includes mechanisms such as reference, ellipsis, lexical cohesion, and conjunctions that ensure continuity and coherence. Maintaining textual cohesion helps in resolving references, identifying missing information through ellipsis, and establishing connections between words and phrases.

5. **Discourse structure:** Discourse structure refers to the organization and hierarchy of information within a discourse. It involves identifying the main ideas, supporting details, and the overall structure of the discourse. Discourse structure helps in understanding the context, identifying key information, and determining the relationships between different parts of the discourse.

Discourse coherence and structure are essential for a range of NLP applications, including text summarization, machine translation, dialogue systems, and information extraction. They contribute to generating more coherent and contextually appropriate responses, improving text understanding, and enhancing the overall quality of language processing outcomes [30].

Researchers in NLP have developed various techniques and models to analyze and generate coherent discourse, including the use of discourse parsers, coherence modeling, discourse-level embeddings, and deep learning architectures. These approaches aim to capture the underlying structure and coherence relations within a discourse, enabling more advanced and accurate language processing capabilities.

5

Natural Language Generation and Machine Translation

Natural language generation (NLG) entails utilizing artificial intelligence (AI) programming to generate written or spoken narratives from a given dataset. NLG is intertwined with both human-to-machine and machine-to-human interaction, encompassing fields such as computational linguistics, natural language processing (NLP), and natural language understanding (NLU).

NLG research often centers on crafting computer programs that contextualize data points. Advanced NLG software can efficiently analyze substantial amounts of numerical data, detect patterns, and communicate these findings in a comprehensible manner for humans. The rapid processing capabilities of NLG software are particularly advantageous for producing time-sensitive content like news articles on the internet. In its optimal form, NLG-generated output can be directly published as web content, maintaining its authenticity and relevance.

Natural language generation (NLG) and machine translation (MT) are two important areas of natural language processing (NLP) that involve creating human-like text in different contexts. While NLG focuses on generating text in a variety of domains and applications, MT specifically deals with translating text from one language to another. Let's explore each of these concepts further: [9]

1. Natural language generation (NLG): Natural language generation is the progression of automatically creating human-like text or speech from structured data or other non-linguistic representations. NLG systems take structured data, such as database records, and transform it into coherent and contextually appropriate human language. NLG finds claims in numerous parts, including chatbots, virtual supporters, personalized recommendations, report generation, and content creation.

NLG techniques involve several components, such as:

- **Content planning:** Determines the overall structure and content of the generated text based on the input data and the desired output.
- **Sentence planning:** Decides how the content will be expressed in sentences, considering factors like sentence structure, vocabulary selection, and grammar.
- **Lexicalization:** Maps the underlying data to appropriate words and phrases based on the chosen sentence structures.
- **Referring expression generation:** Generates raising expressions (e.g., pronouns, definite noun expressions) to refer to entities mentioned in the text.

NLG systems leverage rule-based approaches, template-based methods, statistical models, and increasingly, deep learning techniques to generate coherent and contextually appropriate text.

2. Machine translation (MT): Machine translation involves the involuntary translation of text from one linguistic to another. It aims to bridge the language barrier and enable communication across different linguistic communities. MT systems take input text in a source language and generate equivalent text in a target language.

MT techniques can be categorized into several types:

- **Rule-based MT:** Uses linguistic rules and dictionaries to translate text based on grammar, syntax, and vocabulary of the source and target languages. It requires extensive manual effort in rule creation.
- **Statistical MT:** Relies on large parallel corpora (aligned texts in source and target languages) to learn statistical models and make translations based on probabilistic patterns. This approach involves training algorithms like phrase-based or arithmetical machine translation.
- **Neural machine translation (NMT):** A popular approach in recent years, NMT utilizes neural networks, such as recurrent or transformer replicas, to learn the mapping between source and goal language sequences. NMT models capture contextual information and have shown improved translation quality.

MT systems face challenges related to ambiguity, idiomatic expressions, rare or unseen words, and maintaining the fluency and accuracy of translations. Ongoing research focuses on improving translation quality, domain adaptation, low-resource languages, and integrating advanced techniques like pre-training and transfer learning. [27]

Both NLG and MT are active research areas, with ongoing advancements in deep learning, large-scale language models, and multilingual representations. These advancements aim to enhance the quality and accuracy of generated text, enable more fluent and contextually appropriate translations, and support effective communication across languages.

5.1 Natural Language Generation: System Architecture and Applications

Natural language generation (NLG) involves the creation of natural language descriptions or narratives from structured data. Positioned within the realm of natural language processing (NLP), NLG often collaborates closely with another NLP sub-field known as natural language understanding (NLU). NLU assists in converting unstructured text inputs into structured representations, which can then be utilized by NLG for generating coherent language.

Interestingly, generating language taps into a more intricate aspect of human cognition compared to comprehending it. Analogously, computers may encounter greater challenges when tackling NLG tasks as opposed to NLU tasks. An adept NLG system has the potential to liberate humans from routine writing tasks, accelerate narrative creation, facilitate nearly real-time reporting, and enhance operational efficiency.[29]

5.1.1 Architecture of NLG systems

The fundamental stages of a typical natural language generation (NLG) pipeline (Figure 5.1) include:

1. **Content determination and text planning:** This step involves identifying the pertinent information to convey and structuring it coherently. Often referred to as macro planning or document planning, this phase might source information from a knowledge base. The selection of information needs to account for the objectives and preferences of both the writer and the reader.
2. **Sentence planning:** In this phase, decisions are made on how to divide the information into sentences and paragraphs, ensuring a smooth and coherent narrative flow. Also known as micro planning, this process employs techniques like referring expressions, aggregation, lexicalization, and grammaticalization.
3. **Surface realization:** Generating grammatically correct individual sentences constitutes this step. Here, syntax selection and inflection play a pivotal role in rendering accurate language structures.

4. **Physical presentation:** The generated output can take the form of written or spoken text. This stage handles aspects like articulation, punctuation, and layout, ensuring the final presentation aligns with the intended communication mode.

Figure 5.1: The pipeline architecture of NLG.

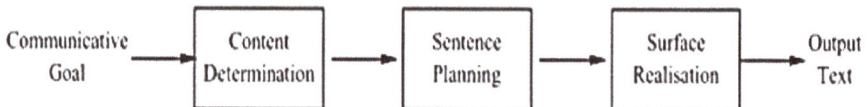

The architecture of NLG systems typically involves several components that work together to transform structured data into coherent and contextually appropriate human language. While different NLG systems may have variations in their architectures, here is a general overview of the components involved:

1. Content planning: Content planning determines the overall structure and content of the generated text. It involves deciding which information to include, the ordering of the information, and the level of detail required. Content planning takes into account the input data, user preferences, system goals, and discourse context.

2. Sentence planning: Sentence planning focuses on how the content will be expressed in sentences. It involves determining the sentence structure, word order, and syntactic transformations. Sentence planning considers factors such as the intended style, tone, and target audience. This component takes the structured data from the content planning phase and converts it into a high-level representation of sentences.

3. Lexicalization: Lexicalization involves mapping the high-level sentence representation to actual words and phrases. It selects appropriate vocabulary, inflects words for grammatical correctness, and applies morphological transformations. Lexicalization also handles issues like determining appropriate tenses, number agreement, and generating appropriate referring expressions.

4. Referring expression generation: Referring expression generation focuses on generating referring expressions such as pronouns, definite noun phrases, or demonstratives. It determines when and how to refer to entities mentioned in the text to ensure coherence and avoid ambiguity. This component considers the discourse context, the salience of different entities, and the conventions of reference in the target language.

5. Realization: The realization component finalizes the generated text by producing the surface form of the sentences. It includes tasks like inflection, determining word order, applying grammatical rules, and adding appropriate punctuation. Realization ensures that the generated text is grammatically correct, coherent, and ready for human consumption.

NLG systems find applications in various domains and use cases, including:

- **Chatbots and virtual assistants:** NLG permits chatbots and virtual supporters to generate responses that are contextually relevant, informative, and engaging.
- **Personalized recommendations:** NLG systems can produce modified recommendations for products, services, or content based on user preferences and historical data.
- **Report generation:** NLG is employed to automatically generate reports, summaries, or insights from structured data, such as financial data, scientific data, or business analytics.
- **Content creation:** NLG systems can generate content for news articles, weather reports, sports summaries, or other forms of informational content.
- **Language tutoring:** NLG can be used to provide interactive language tutoring by generating exercises, prompts, and feedback tailored to learners' needs.
- **Accessibility tools:** NLG can assist individuals with visual impairments by converting visual information into text or generating audio descriptions of visual content.

NLG is a rapidly evolving field, with ongoing research focusing on improving language fluency, generating more diverse and creative text, incorporating deep learning techniques, and addressing challenges like generating explanations and handling dialogue-based interactions.

5.1.2 Applications of NLG

There is a wide array of practical applications for natural language generation (NLG):

Businesses employ NLG for generating analysis reports in areas like business intelligence dashboards, IoT device status and maintenance reporting, personalized client financial portfolio summaries, and personalized customer communications. It also plays a fundamental role alongside natural language understanding (NLU) in the functioning of chatbots and voice assistants.

A familiar instance is Gmail's Smart Compose, which suggests concise email responses by analyzing email content. The Associated Press utilizes NLG to generate thousands of corporate earnings reports rapidly. During the December 2019 UK elections, BBC News utilized NLG to publish numerous localized articles in a matter of hours, adapting content style and tone to suit local audiences.

In the computer science domain, NLG has been applied to tasks such as generating specifications from UML diagrams or describing changes in source code.

Forge.ai, facing data limitations for supervised NLU models, harnessed NLG to synthesize training data. Similarly, synthesized electronic health records facilitate sharing de-identified data among healthcare providers and training machine learning models.

Industries spanning finance, human resources, legal, marketing, sales, operations, strategy, and supply chain stand to benefit from NLG. Specific sectors such as financial services, pharmaceuticals and healthcare, media and entertainment, retail, manufacturing, and logistics can greatly leverage NLG.

Some of the most common NLG applications include:

- **Analytics reporting:** NLG aids in generating accessible reports from analyzed data, providing actionable insights and facilitating decision-making.
- **Content automation:** NLG automates content generation for various textual communications, enhancing standardization, accuracy, and turnaround time.
- **Virtual assistants and chatbots:** Popular virtual assistants use NLG to generate context-specific responses for effective customer interaction and problem-solving.
- **Risk management:** NLG assists in risk assessment, compliance management, fraud detection, and anti-money laundering.
- **Customer experience:** NLG enhances customer care procedures by delivering personalized and accurate responses to inquiries and complaints.
- **Automated journalism:** NLG contributes to the automated creation of news articles and reports.
- **Data-driven insights:** NLG enables businesses to extract insights from big data, thereby increasing revenue and expanding analytic output.
- **Finance and banking:** NLG automates performance and profit-loss reporting, and aids fintech chatbots in providing financial management advice.
- **Manufacturing:** NLG automates communication of critical data from IoT devices for performance enhancement and maintenance reporting.

Overall, NLG empowers businesses with enhanced data analysis, quicker insights, improved customer interaction, and automation of various processes.

Natural language generation (NLG) has an extensive variety of submissions crosswise numerous areas. Some of the prominent applications of NLG include:

1. Automated report generation: NLG systems can automatically generate reports based on structured data. This is particularly useful in fields such as finance, business analytics, and data-driven industries, where large amounts of data need to be transformed into readable and actionable reports. NLG can summarize trends, highlight key insights, and present data in a clear and concise manner.

2. Chatbots and virtual assistants: NLG plays a crucial role in enabling chatbots and virtual assistants to generate human-like responses. NLG systems can generate dynamic and contextually appropriate messages based on user queries or actions. Chatbots with NLG capabilities can engage in conversational interactions, provide personalized recommendations, answer questions, and assist users in various tasks.

3. E-commerce and personalized recommendations: NLG can enhance e-commerce platforms by generating product descriptions, personalized recommendations, and product reviews. NLG systems can create engaging and persuasive descriptions of products, taking into account user preferences, past interactions, and other relevant data to deliver customized recommendations.

4. News generation: NLG systems are used to automatically generate news articles or summaries. These systems can analyze data sources, extract key information, and generate coherent news stories. NLG in news generation can be applied to areas such as financial news, sports updates, weather reports, and other data-driven news domains.

5. Content creation: NLG can automate content creation for various purposes. It can generate social media posts, blog articles, marketing copy, and other forms of written content. NLG systems can adapt to different tones, styles, and target audiences, allowing for efficient content generation and distribution.

6. Language tutoring and education: NLG can be utilized in language tutoring and education applications. It can generate exercises, prompts, and personalized feedback for learners. NLG systems can provide language learners with interactive exercises, grammar explanations, vocabulary suggestions, and language practice opportunities.

7. Accessibility tools: NLG can aid individuals with visual impairments by converting visual information into text or generating audio descriptions. NLG systems can describe images, charts, graphs, and other visual content, making it accessible to those who cannot perceive visual information directly.

8. Data analytics and business intelligence: NLG can assist in interpreting and communicating insights from complex data analytics. By automatically generating narratives, NLG systems can explain trends, anomalies, and patterns in data, making it easier for decision-makers to understand and act upon the findings.

These are just a few examples of the many applications of NLG. NLG continues to advance, leveraging methods such as deep learning and natural language understanding to generate more sophisticated and contextually appropriate text in various domains.

5.2 Machine Translation: Challenges and Approaches

Machine translation (MT) is a stimulating task in natural language processing (NLP), and it faces several problems that affect the quality and accuracy of translations. Some common problems in machine translation include:

1. Ambiguity: Language is inherently ambiguous, and machine translation systems often struggle to disambiguate words, phrases, and sentences. Ambiguities can arise due to lexical ambiguity (multiple meanings of words), syntactic ambiguity (multiple possible parse trees), or semantic ambiguity (multiple possible interpretations). Resolving these ambiguities accurately is a difficult task for MT systems, leading to potential errors in translations.

2. Idiomatic expressions and collocations: Idiomatic expressions, phrasal verbs, and collocations pose challenges for machine translation. These linguistic constructions have non-literal meanings that are difficult to translate directly. MT systems may struggle to recognize and accurately render these expressions, resulting in literal or incorrect translations.

3. Rare or unseen words: MT systems often encounter words or phrases that are rare or unseen in the training data. Translating such words becomes challenging as there may be limited or no contextual information available. Additionally, out-of-vocabulary (OOV) words, such as proper nouns or domain-specific terms, can lead to incorrect translations or the use of generic placeholders.

4. Morphological variations: Languages exhibit rich morphological variations, including inflections, conjugations, and declensions. MT systems need to handle these variations accurately to generate grammatically correct translations. However, capturing and generating the appropriate morphological forms for different languages is a complex task, and errors can occur, especially in agglutinative or highly inflected languages.

5. Syntax and word order: Word order varies across languages, and translating the syntactic structure accurately is a major challenge in MT. Some languages have flexible word orders, while others have strict rules. Maintaining the correct word order and preserving the intended meaning can be difficult, leading to unnatural or ungrammatical translations.

6. Domain adaptation: MT systems trained on general-purpose data may struggle when translating domain-specific content. Domain-specific terminology, jargon, or specialized language may not be adequately covered in the training data. Adapting MT systems to specific domains or fine-tuning them for specific tasks can help mitigate this problem.

7. Cultural and contextual nuances: Translations often require consideration of cultural and contextual nuances that are specific to a language or region. MT systems may struggle to capture these nuances, leading to translations that are accurate in terms of literal meaning but may lack cultural appropriateness or fail to convey the intended meaning in the target language.

Addressing these challenges requires ongoing research and development in machine translation. Researchers are exploring approaches such as neural machine translation (NMT), transfer learning, domain adaptation, and leveraging large-scale multilingual models to improve translation quality, handle ambiguity, and capture contextual and cultural nuances. Additionally, the integration of post-editing by human translators or advanced interactive translation systems can assistance refine and recover the output of machine translation systems.

5.2.1 Issues in machine translation

Advancements in technology have revolutionized the field of translation, offering machine translation software that can swiftly translate entire documents with minimal cost. However, before dismissing human translators in favor of these tools, it's important to recognize several challenges that machine translation faces, which can be addressed effectively by human translators.

1. **Quality challenges:** Machine translation encounters significant quality issues due to its inability to comprehend contextual nuances. While computers struggle to grasp the contextual intricacies of language, humans excel at understanding emotions, non-verbal cues, and cultural subtleties that significantly impact language context. This deficiency leads to translation errors, especially in complex scenarios, where human translators' contextual understanding shines.

2. **Lack of feedback and collaboration:** Although virtual assistants like Siri simulate intelligent interaction, they lack true collaboration capabilities. Machine translation software cannot provide real-time feedback or collaborate effectively with users. This limitation impedes obtaining insights for crucial tasks like translating marketing content for global product launches. Collaborating with a professional translation firm allows for tailored and precise translations, enabling informed decision-making.

3. **Absence of creativity:** Language mastery requires creativity, honed through extensive exposure and practice. While machine translation handles straightforward content adequately, it fails to capture the artistic and creative aspects of language. Successful business communication, especially with global partners and clients, demands creativity that only skilled human translators can deliver.

4. **Cultural insensitivity:** Each culture embodies unique values and norms, influencing communication styles. Machine translation lacks the cultural sensitivity required to navigate these intricacies, potentially causing misunderstandings or even offense. Human translators, familiar with cultural norms, ensure accurate and culturally sensitive translations, minimizing business risks.

5. **Cost considerations:** Opting for free or cheap machine translation may lead to subpar quality. Quality work demands adequate investment, as rushed translations often compromise accuracy and effectiveness.

6. **Importance of time and attention:** High-quality work necessitates time, care, and attention. Swift completion is often indicative of compromised quality. Thus, relying on human translators ensures meticulous attention to detail and optimal results.

7. **Contextual coherence:** Machine translation may interpret the same term differently across document sections, resulting in inconsistencies. Human translators maintain consistent terminology throughout a project, preventing confusion for readers.

8. **Security concerns:** The security of data inputted into free machine translation solutions is questionable, as these open-access tools may lack robust data protection. Opting for reputable translation system vendors is crucial to safeguard sensitive information.

9. **Formatting Challenges:** Complex formatting poses difficulties for machine translation, potentially segmenting text inappropriately and disrupting context. Human translators ensure that formatting is preserved and text remains coherent.

In conclusion, while machine translation offers convenience, its limitations in understanding context, collaborating, delivering creativity, and cultural sensitivity make human translators invaluable for ensuring high-quality, accurate, and contextually appropriate translations. Business success in global markets hinges on the expertise and experience of human translators in bridging linguistic and cultural gaps.

Machine translation (MT) is a challenging task in natural language processing (NLP), and it faces several problems that affect the quality and accuracy of translations. Some common problems in machine translation include:

1. Ambiguity: Language is inherently ambiguous, and machine translation systems often struggle to disambiguate words, phrases, and sentences. Ambiguities can arise due to lexical ambiguity (multiple meanings of words), syntactic ambiguity (multiple possible parse trees), or semantic ambiguity (multiple possible interpretations). Resolving these ambiguities accurately is a difficult task for MT systems, leading to potential errors in translations.

2. Idiomatic expressions and collocations: Idiomatic expressions, phrasal verbs, and collocations pose challenges for machine translation. These linguistic constructions have non-literal meanings that are difficult to translate directly. MT systems may struggle to recognize and accurately render these expressions, resulting in literal or incorrect translations.

3. Rare or unseen words: MT systems often encounter words or phrases that are rare or unseen in the training data. Translating such words becomes challenging as there may be limited or no contextual information available. Additionally, out-of-vocabulary (OOV) words, such as proper nouns or domain-specific terms, can lead to incorrect translations or the use of generic placeholders.

4. Morphological variations: Languages exhibit rich morphological variations, including inflections, conjugations, and declensions. MT systems need to handle these variations accurately to generate grammatically correct translations. However, capturing and generating the appropriate morphological forms for different languages is a complex task, and errors can occur, especially in agglutinative or highly inflected languages.

5. Syntax and word order: Word order varies across languages, and translating the syntactic structure accurately is a major challenge in MT. Some languages have flexible word orders, while others have strict rules. Maintaining the correct word order and preserving the intended meaning can be difficult, leading to unnatural or ungrammatical translations.

6. Domain adaptation: MT systems trained on general-purpose data may struggle when translating domain-specific content. Domain-specific terminology, jargon, or specialized language may not be adequately covered in the training data. Adapting MT systems to specific domains or fine-tuning them for specific tasks can help mitigate this problem.

7. Cultural and contextual nuances: Translations often require consideration of cultural and contextual nuances that are specific to a language or region. MT systems may struggle to capture these nuances, leading to translations that are accurate in terms of literal meaning but may lack cultural appropriateness or fail to convey the intended meaning in the target language.

Addressing these challenges requires ongoing research and development in machine translation. Researchers are exploring approaches such as neural machine translation (NMT), transfer learning, domain adaptation, and leveraging large-scale multilingual models to improve translation quality, handle ambiguity, and capture contextual and cultural nuances. Additionally, the integration of post-editing by human translators or advanced interactive translation systems can help refine and improve the output of machine translation systems.

5.3 Diverse approaches to machine translation

Machine translation (MT) approaches have evolved over the years, with various techniques and models developed to improve translation quality. Here are some prominent approaches in machine translation:

1. Rule-based machine translation (RBMT): Rule-based machine translation utilizes language rules and dictionaries to interpret text from the foundation language to the goal language. These rules are crafted by linguists and language experts and include grammar rules, syntactic patterns, and lexical information. RBMT systems often rely on handcrafted linguistic resources and extensive human effort to create and maintain the rule sets. While RBMT can handle linguistic phenomena and domain-specific knowledge effectively, it can be labor-intensive and may struggle with capturing language variations and handling rare or unseen words.

2. Statistical machine translation (SMT): Statistical machine translation uses statistical models to learn patterns and relationships between source and target language text from parallel corpora, which are aligned texts in the source and target languages. SMT models employ techniques like phrase-based translation, where translations are generated based on statistical probabilities of phrases or sub-phrases occurring in the training data. SMT models also leverage language models to capture the fluency of translations. SMT systems require large amounts of parallel data for training and often rely on statistical algorithms for decoding. While SMT has been widely used and successful, it can struggle with capturing long-range dependencies and handling rare or unseen words.

3. Neural machine translation (NMT): Neural machine translation is a more recent and popular approach that employs artificial neural networks to learn the mapping between source and target language text. NMT models, such as recurrent neural networks (RNNs) or transformer models, take advantage of their ability to capture contextual information effectively. NMT models can handle long-range dependencies, capture syntactic and semantic relationships, and produce fluent translations. They are trained end-to-end, optimizing the translation quality directly. NMT has shown significant improvements in translation accuracy and is widely adopted in many state-of-the-art MT systems.

4. Hybrid approaches: Hybrid approaches combine different MT techniques to leverage their strengths and mitigate their weaknesses. For example, a hybrid system may use RBMT to handle specific linguistic phenomena or domain-specific knowledge, while employing statistical or neural models for the bulk of the translation. Hybrid systems aim to achieve better translation quality by combining the advantages of different approaches.

5. Transfer learning and pre-trained models: Transfer learning and pre-trained representations have gained popularity in MT. Large-scale pre-trained language models, such as the transformer-based models like BERT (bidirectional encoder representations from transformers) or GPT (generative pre-trained transformer), are fine-tuned on translation tasks. These models learn representations of language that capture context, semantics, and syntactic structures, and can be used as a starting point for training MT systems. Transfer learning allows models to generalize across languages and tasks, reducing the need for extensive language-specific training data.

These approaches continue to evolve, with ongoing research focusing on improvements in translation quality, addressing specific challenges, and incorporating techniques like domain adaptation, low-resource translation, multimodal translation, and advanced decoding algorithms. Additionally, techniques like interactive translation, where human translators and MT systems collaborate, are also being explored to enhance translation quality and productivity.

Machine translation (MT) techniques can be categorized based on their underlying principles. Two prominent approaches are rule-based and corpus-based machine translation. Rule-based MT involves linguistic analysis of source and target languages, while corpus-based MT relies on bilingual text corpora for translation. These methodologies reflect rationalism and empiricism, respectively.

1. **Rule-based vs. corpus-based:** Rule-based machine translation (RBMT) employs linguistic rules to analyze morphological, syntactic, and semantic aspects of both languages. It can provide reasonable quality translations using well-defined rules, but constructing such systems is time-consuming and labor-intensive due to manual crafting of linguistic resources.

    In contrast, corpus-based machine translation (CBMT) relies on bilingual text corpora and machine learning. It learns from parallel texts, either through specific examples or statistical probabilities, to generate translations. CBMT is more data-driven, adaptable, and less dependent on manually crafted rules.

2. **Direct, transfer, and interlingual translation:** These approaches, existing within RBMT, differ in the depth of source language analysis and the extent of achieving language-independent representation of meaning between source and target languages. They are represented in the Vauquois Triangle, illustrating analysis levels.

    - **Direct translation (DT):** This involves word-level translation and simple grammar adjustments. DT seeks direct correspondences between lexical units of source and target languages, offering quick but shallow translations.
    - **Transfer-based translation (TBT):** Comprising analysis, conversion, and generation stages, TBT uses language-specific representations for translation. It balances efficiency and language independence.
    - **Interlingual translation (ILT):** Replaces transfer with interlingua, a universal language-independent meaning representation. ILT has analysis and synthesis phases, offering a trade-off between cost and complexity. However, defining an interlingua is challenging.

3. **Statistical and example-based translation:** These methods fall under CBMT, utilizing bilingual corpora for learning.

    - **Statistical machine translation (SMT):** Parameters derived from bilingual corpora drive SMT models. Translations are based on the most probable option according to statistical analysis. The Bayes theorem is commonly used. SMT is data-driven, needing preprocessing and possibly yielding non-identical translations for the same input.
    - **Example-based machine translation (EBMT):** EBMT relies on bilingual parallel texts, emphasizing analogy-based translation. Four tasks involve example acquisition, management, application, and synthesis. EBMT and SMT share characteristics like data-driven learning, adaptability, and the potential for new language pairs.

In summary, the distinctions between rule-based and corpus-based approaches lie in manual rules vs. data-driven learning. Within RBMT, direct, transfer, and interlingual approaches differ in depth of source language analysis. In CBMT, statistical and example-based methods use bilingual corpora for learning, varying in how they leverage data for translation.

5.4 Evaluating Machine Translation Systems

The evaluation of machine translation (MT) systems is crucial to assess their translation quality and compare different approaches. Various evaluation metrics and methodologies have been developed to measure the performance of MT systems. Here are some common evaluation approaches:

1. Human evaluation: Human evaluation involves having human judges assess the quality of paraphrases fashioned by MT schemes. This can be done through different methods, such as:

- **Manual assessment:** Human evaluators rate translations based on different criteria, such as fluency (grammatical correctness), adequacy (faithfulness to the source meaning), and overall quality. They may also provide feedback on specific aspects of the translation.
- **Comparative evaluation:** Human evaluators compare translations produced by different MT systems or compare MT translations to human reference translations. They rank or rate translations based on quality, preference, or similarity to the reference.

Human evaluation is considered the gold standard as it captures the subjective aspects of translation quality. However, it can be time-consuming, expensive, and subjective due to inter-annotator variability.

2. Automatic evaluation metrics: Automatic evaluation metrics provide a faster and cost-effective way to assess MT system performance. These metrics rely on comparison the production of the MT system to reference translations or human judgments. Some widely used automatic evaluation metrics include:

- **BLEU (bilingual evaluation understudy):** BLEU measures the similarity between MT output and one or more reference translations. It compares N-gram overlap and considers precision and brevity penalties. BLEU is widely used but has limitations, such as being sensitive to word order and vocabulary mismatch.
- **METEOR (metric for evaluation of translation with explicit ordering):** METEOR is another popular metric that reflects precision, recall, and alignment-based measures. It incorporates various linguistic and semantic matching techniques, such as stemming, synonymy, and paraphrase matching.

- **TER (translation edit rate):** TER calculates the number of edits (insertions, deletions, substitutions) required to transform the MT output into a reference translation. It focuses on edit distance and can be useful for evaluating fluency and adequacy.
- **NIST (National Institute of Standards and Technology):** NIST metric is similar to BLEU but employs a weighted combination of N-gram precision scores.

Automatic evaluation metrics provide quick and objective measurements of translation quality. However, they have limitations in capturing all aspects of translation quality, such as fluency, adequacy, and contextual appropriateness.

3. Error analysis: Error analysis involves identifying and categorizing errors made by MT systems to gain insights into their strengths and weaknesses. This can be done by manually examining a sample set of translations and identifying specific types of errors, such as grammatical errors, missing information, or incorrect word choices. Error analysis helps in identifying areas of improvement and guiding the development of MT systems.

4. User feedback and preference: User feedback and preference can deliver valued visions into the usability and acceptability of MT systems. This can be obtained through user surveys, user ratings, or user studies where individuals interact with the translations produced by MT systems and provide feedback on their quality, usefulness, and user experience.

It's significant to note that a combination of assessment approaches is often used to comprehensively assess MT systems. Each evaluation approach has its strengths and limitations, and a holistic evaluation provides a more complete understanding of the translation quality. Furthermore, evaluation criteria may vary depending on the specific application and use circumstance of the MT system.

1.Human evaluation: Various methods have been employed to evaluate machine translation systems, aiming to assess their output quality. Some of these evaluation methodologies include:

1. **Automatic Language Processing Advisory Committee (ALPAC):** The ALPAC report conducted a study comparing human translation with machine translation output. Trained human judges evaluated translations based on "intelligibility" and "fidelity." Intelligibility measured sentence understandability on a scale of 1–9, while fidelity assessed information retention compared to the original. Intelligibility was rated independently, while fidelity was indirectly evaluated by presenting judges with translated text followed by the original.
Results indicated strong correlation between the two variables when averaged per sentence. Judges' variation was minimal, recommending at least three or four raters. This methodology effectively differentiated human and machine translations.

2. **Advanced Research Projects Agency (ARPA):** Under the Human Language Technologies Program, ARPA established a comprehensive evaluation methodology for machine translation systems. Different approaches (statistical, rule-based, and human-assisted) were tested. Methods including comprehension evaluation, quality panel evaluation, and adequacy and fluency evaluation were explored.

   Comprehension evaluation compared systems through multiple-choice comprehension tests, but was abandoned due to meaning modification in translations. Quality panel evaluation was complex to arrange. Adequacy and fluency evaluation gained prominence, involving monolingual judges rating document segments for information transfer (adequacy) and linguistic fluency.

3. **Automatic evaluation metrics:** Automated metrics were developed to quantitatively evaluate machine translation output.

   - **BLEU (bilingual evaluation understudy):** This correlated well with human judgment. BLEU computes scores for individual segments, usually sentences, and averages them across the corpus. It calculates precision modified to address word inflation in machine translations.
   - **NIST (National Institute of Standards and Technology):** A derivative of BLEU, NIST incorporates informative N-gram weights and adjusts for translation length variations.
   - **METEOR (metric for evaluation of translation with explicit ordering):** METEOR addresses BLEU's limitations by employing unigram precision and recall harmonic mean. It considers synonyms and incorporates stemmers for matching flexibility.
   - **LEPOR:** LEPOR is a novel evaluation metric that combines existing and modified factors, including precision, recall, sentence-length penalty, and N-gram-based word order penalty. Showed improved correlation with human judgments compared to other metrics in experimental evaluations.

These evaluation methods provide tools to assess machine translation output quality in various ways, offering insights into their effectiveness and allowing researchers to refine and improve translation systems.

5.5 Case Study: Unique Features of Indian Languages

Introduction: India is a linguistically diverse country, with hundreds of languages spoken across its regions. In this case study, we will explore some common characteristics of Indian languages that distinguish them from other language families. Indian languages exhibit several unique characteristics that set them apart from other languages. Here are some prominent characteristics of Indian languages:

1. Language families: Indian languages belong to various language families, including Indo-Aryan, Dravidian, Austroasiatic, Tibeto-Burman, and others. Indo-Aryan languages, such as Hindi, Bengali, Punjabi, and Gujarati, and are the most widely spoken language families in India. Dravidian languages, including Tamil, Telugu, Kannada, and Malayalam, have a significant presence in South India. Each language family has its own distinct features, grammar, and vocabulary.

2. Phonetics and phonology: Indian languages have rich phonetic inventories with a wide range of consonants and vowels. Many languages distinguish between aspirated and unaspirated consonants, retroflex consonants, and nasalized vowels. Some languages, like Tamil, have unique phonetic features like the use of Grantha letters, which are special characters used for writing Sanskrit loanwords.

3. Writing systems: Indian languages have diverse writing systems. Devanagari script is widely used for writing Indo-Aryan languages like Hindi, Marathi, and Sanskrit. Other scripts include Bengali script, Tamil script, Telugu script, Kannada script, and more. Some languages have multiple scripts associated with them, and the choice of script may vary based on region or community.

4. Verb structure: Indian languages often exhibit complex verb structures. Verbs are conjugated to reflect tense, aspect, mood, person, and number. They may also indicate honorific forms to show respect or politeness. Some Indian languages have a rich system of verb agreement with subjects, objects, and other grammatical elements.

5. Honorifics and politeness: Indian languages have elaborate systems of honorifics and politeness markers. Different verb forms, pronouns, and vocabulary are used to show respect or politeness based on social relationships, hierarchical positions, and age differences.

6. Diglossia and code-switching: Many Indian languages exhibit diglossia, where a formal or literary variant of the language coexists with a spoken or colloquial variant. This diglossic situation is commonly observed in languages like Hindi, Tamil, and Bengali. Code-switching, the mixing of two or more languages within a conversation, is also prevalent in multilingual Indian contexts.

7. Compound words and agglutination: Indian languages often have a tendency to form compound words by combining multiple roots or morphemes. Compounding allows for the creation of new words and facilitates expressiveness. Additionally, Indian languages frequently employ agglutination, where affixes or suffixes are added to a root word to convey various grammatical information.

8. Influence of Sanskrit: Sanskrit, a classical language of ancient India, has had a profound influence on many Indian languages. Numerous words, idioms, and grammatical structures in Indian languages have roots in Sanskrit. Sanskrit has also contributed to the development of technical, scientific, and philosophical vocabulary.

It's important to note that these characteristics vary across different Indian languages and are influenced by regional, cultural, and historical factors. India's linguistic diversity makes it a linguistically rich and fascinating country, with each language having its own unique features and beauty.

The characteristics of Indian languages highlight their diversity and complexity. From the multitude of language families to the diverse writing systems, phonetic intricacies, rich morphology, and social language norms, Indian languages showcase the linguistic wealth of the country. Understanding these characteristics is crucial for effective language processing and development of language technologies tailored to the Indian context.

Indian languages exhibit distinct features in their phoneme sets, scripts, reduplication, and onomatopoeic expressions:

1. **Phoneme set:** Phonemes serve as the foundational elements of linguistic analysis, particularly within the domain of phonology. In the context of Indian languages, phonemes are pivotal units that differentiate meanings among words. Unlike alphabetic scripts where individual letters represent distinct sounds, phonemes in Indian languages often correspond to syllables or clusters of sounds. For instance, in languages like Hindi or Tamil, a single phoneme might comprise a consonant–vowel combination (CV) or even a consonant cluster followed by a vowel. This nuanced comprehension of phonemes is crucial for accurately transcribing and comprehending spoken language, as it captures the intricate phonetic details inherent in Indian linguistic systems. Additionally, the phoneme set in Indian languages may encompass unique features such as retroflex consonants, nasalized vowels, and distinct intonation patterns, further enriching the complexity of their phonological systems.
2. **Distinct graphemes:** Although the Indian languages share a common alphabet, their scripts have distinct graphemes for printing. India has 10–12 major scripts. Devanagari, used for Hindi, Marathi, Konkani, and Nepali, is the most widespread. Different scripts have varied

approaches to grapheme design and combination. Scripts may include head-lines, non-touching graphemes, and modified forms of consonants for vowels. Samyuktakshara's supporting consonants can be modifier graphemes with unique positions relative to the main one.

3. **Reduplication:** Reduplication is a notable feature in Indian languages, used for diverse functions. The subcontinent features various reduplicative expressions. Echo formations, related to reduplication, are also significant. Dravidian languages often employ echo formations. These linguistic traits add depth to the languages' expressive capabilities.

4. **Onomatopoeic expressions:** Onomatopoeic expressions and expressive forms share common traits, where neither part independently holds meaning. Contrastingly, the base of an echo expression forms a lexical item itself. Indian languages show a fondness for onomatopoeic expressions. These expressions might or might not be reduplicated in structure, allowing for exact repetition or segmental variations.

These linguistic characteristics showcase the richness and diversity of Indian languages, each adding depth and nuance to communication and expression.

(*) kiiccukiiccu-n nu	—	'chirping'	(TAMIL)
taaraa zuvva,	—	'like a star'	(TELUGU)
sura-sura batti	—	'sparklers',	(HINDI)
kaakara-puvvu-vatti	—	'sparklers'	(TELUGU)
kora kora choochu	—	'frowning'	(TELUGU)
kasa kasa namulu	—	chewing'	(TELUGU)
gora gora gunju	—	(probably only in our telangANA dists.)	

1. **Expressive**: The following category exhibits numerous parallels with onomatopoeic expressions, although it encompasses terms that aren't strictly sound symbolic. Unlike onomatopoeics and expressives, these terms extend beyond positive utterances. Here are illustrative examples of expressives from Hindi, Telugu, and Bengali:

Chi chi	—	'dirty, filthy'	(Telugu)
chip chip	—	'sticky'	(Hindi)
thik thik	—	'sense of teeming with maggots'	(Bengali)
pil pil	—	'sense of being overcrowded'	(Bengali)
Rama rama	—	'expressing disgust'	(Telugu)
Kani kani	—	' wait / let us see what happens next '	(Telugu)

2. **Paired words**: These instances entail the combination of two lexical elements and are commonly denoted in academic discourse as "synonymic compounds," "synonymic repetition," "semantic reduplication," and "redundant compounds." Both components belong to the same

realm of meaning and can assume several potential relationships with each other.

tikku ticai	—	'point of direction direction' i.e. 'direction'	(Tamil)
kuti makkal	—	'subjects children' i.e. 'citizens'	(Tamil)
taay takappan	—	'mother father' i.e. 'parents'	(Tamil)
pilla jalla	—	'children'	(Telugu)

Parallel examples of each type can be given for Hindi.

dhan daulat 'wealth wealth' i.e. 'wealth, riches'

saanii paanii 'cattle-cake water' i.e. 'cattle'

raat din or din raat 'night day' i.e. 'continually'

Paired synonyms often encompass words drawn from distinct registers, dialects, or even languages.

3. **Echo**: Echo expressions, also referred to as "echo words" or "echo formations," constitute another category of reduplicated forms. Their semantic structure falls between onomatopoeics and expressives, where neither component holds independent meaning, and paired words and instances of complete syntactic reduplication, where both parts can have distinct meanings. The base of an echo formation, predominantly appearing first, is always a standalone lexical item, while the reduplicated part lacks autonomous lexical significance. Echo expressions consistently exhibit a cluster of meanings across languages, differentiating them from other parts of the linguistic continuum. However, significant variation exists within echo expressions, impacting considerations of lexical storage.

Diverse languages exhibit preferences for distinct fixed segments, such as ki(i)-/gi(i)- in Dravidian languages. Echo expressions with distinctive phonology and potential semantics are prevalent in the Indian subcontinent. Such formations are notably productive. For instance, in Telugu, younger speakers tend to create sentences like:

uppu cappu	—	'taste'	(Telugu)
illu gillu	—	'house'	(Telugu)
ekkada akkada	—	'here and there'	(Telugu)
kaappi kiippi	—	'coffee and other beverages'	(Tamil)
paampu kiimpu	—	'snakes and other reptiles/pests'	(Tamil)
puli kili	—	'Tiger and such like animal'	(Tamil)
Aisa Waisa	—	' this way that way'	(Hindi)
Eidhar Udhar	—	' here or there'	(Hindi)

"Pelli ayindi kaani gilli avaleedu," which translates to "The marriage took place but not gilli (the consummation)."

Another Dravidian example, this time from Malayalam, showcases metalinguistic usage:

"ummaan ko uttaal ammaavan alle kil kimmaavan," which can be understood as "As long as he feeds me, he's called 'Uncle', but otherwise 'Kincle'."

Although a marginal phenomenon, this represents a potential evolution from echo expressions, where the two halves begin to diverge. Echo words often carry scornful or sarcastic connotations, a meaning observed across various languages. Another interpretation is that echo expressions merely intensify or emphasize the base word's meaning. These expressions encode the speaker's affective state, encompassing emotions directed towards the addressee or the described subject. This includes emotions like playfulness, hesitation, ridicule, and emphatic negation.

6

Information Retrieval and Lexical Resources

Information retrieval (IR) refers to a software application designed to manage, store, retrieve, and assess information from collections of documents, primarily focusing on textual content. This system aids users in locating the information they seek, although it doesn't directly provide answers to queries. Instead, it indicates the presence and whereabouts of documents that potentially contain the desired information. These documents that meet the user's needs are termed relevant documents. An ideal IR system would exclusively retrieve documents that are pertinent to the user's query.

Figure 6.1 illustrates the process wherein a user seeking information must formulate a query in natural language. The information retrieval (IR) system then responds by retrieving relevant documents containing the required information [15].

One of the classical problems within information retrieval is the ad-hoc retrieval problem. In ad-hoc retrieval, users input natural language queries to describe the information they need. Subsequently, the IR system returns documents related to the requested information. This process can sometimes yield non-relevant pages alongside relevant ones, leading to the ad-hoc retrieval problem.

The IR model serves as a predictive tool to anticipate and explain the information a user will find based on their query. This model encompasses:

- A document model
- A query model
- A matching function that compares queries to documents

Figure 6.1: The development of information retrieval (IR).

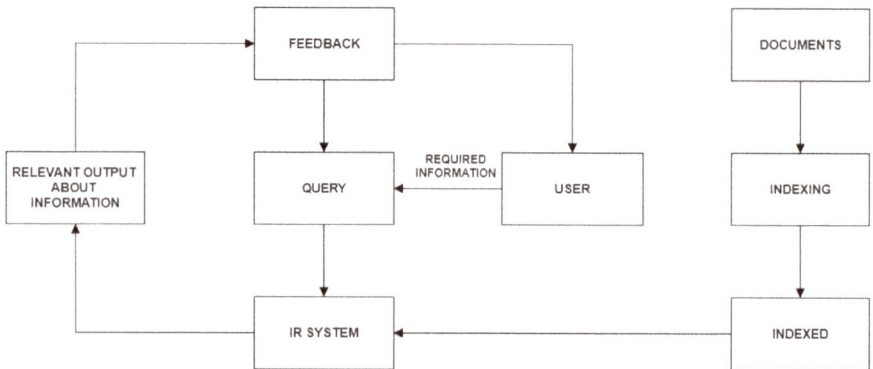

- Mathematically, a retrieval model consists of three components:

D: Representation for documents
R: Representation for queries
F: The modeling framework for D and Q along with their relationship R(q, di), a similarity function ranking documents with respect to the query, also known as ranking.

There are various types of IR models, including classical IR models, non-classical IR models, and alternative IR models.

Design features of information retrieval systems include:

Inverted index: A primary data structure representing most IR systems, listing documents containing specific words along with their frequencies.

Stop word elimination: Removal of high-frequency, semantically insignificant words known as stop words to reduce the size of the inverted index.

Stemming: A heuristic process to extract base forms of words by removing word endings.

The Boolean model: The oldest IR model based on set theory and Boolean algebra, using operators like AND, OR, and NOT to construct queries.

Vector space model: A model that overcomes some limitations of the Boolean model by representing documents and queries as vectors in a high-dimensional space and using cosine similarity for ranking.

Advantages of the Boolean model:

- Simplicity based on sets
- Easy to understand and implement
- User has a sense of control,

Disadvantages of the Boolean model:

- Lack of partial matches
- Strong influence of Boolean operators
- Complex query language
- No ranking for retrieved documents.

Overall, the information retrieval process involves multiple steps within the NLP pipeline, including tokenization and normalization of text. The tokenization process divides text into words or sentences using functions like word tokenize and sent_tokenize from the nltk.tokenize module. The goal is to facilitate the organization, storage, retrieval, and evaluation of textual information to meet users' information needs.

6.1 Information Retrieval: Design Aspects of Retrieval Systems

Information retrieval systems are designed to efficiently and effectively retrieve relevant information from a collection of documents or data sources. These systems can be classified into different categories based on their design features. There are three primary categories in which information retrieval (IR) models can be classified:

1. Classical IR model: The classical IR model is straightforward and simple to implement. It relies on mathematical principles that are widely recognized and easily comprehensible. Within this category, there are three subtypes: Boolean, vector, and probabilistic models.

2. Non-classical IR model: In contrast to the classical IR model, the non-classical IR model is founded on principles other than similarity, probability, and Boolean operations. This category of model explores alternative approaches to information retrieval. Examples of non-classical IR models include the information logic model, situation theory model, and interaction models.

3. Alternative IR model: The alternative IR model builds upon the foundation of the classical IR model by incorporating techniques from other fields to enhance its capabilities. This category includes models like the cluster model, fuzzy model, and latent semantic indexing (LSI) model, which leverage ideas from other domains to improve information retrieval performance [23].

1. Classical information retrieval systems:

Query-based retrieval: Classical systems typically use query-based retrieval, where users input their information needs in the form of a query. The system matches the query against the documents in the collection and returns the most relevant results.

Boolean retrieval: Classical systems often employ Boolean retrieval models, where queries consist of Boolean operators (AND, OR, NOT) to combine terms and specify relationships between them.

Exact matching: Classical systems primarily focus on exact term matching, where the retrieval is based on matching the query terms exactly with the terms in the documents.

Inverted index: Classical systems commonly utilize an reversed index, which is a data structure that maps terms to the documents in which they appear. This allows for efficient term-based retrieval.

2. Non-classical information retrieval systems:

Probabilistic retrieval: Non-classical systems employ probabilistic retrieval models, such as the probabilistic relevance model or language models. These models estimate the probability of relevance between a document and a query, allowing for ranking of results based on relevance probabilities.

Vector space model: Non-classical systems often represent papers and queries as courses in a high-dimensional space, where each dimension resembles to a term. Similarity measures, such as cosine similarity, are used to rank credentials based on their similarity to the query.

Ranked retrieval: Non-classical systems typically employ ranked retrieval, where documents are ranked according to their relevance scores or probabilities. The top-ranked documents are then presented to the user.

Partial matching: Non-classical systems may incorporate techniques for partial matching or fuzzy matching, where documents that contain variations or synonyms of the query terms are also considered.

3. Alternative information retrieval systems:

Concept-based retrieval: Alternative systems focus on retrieving documents founded on their conceptual sense rather than exact keyword similar. These systems employ techniques such as semantic analysis, topic modeling, or natural language processing to understand the underlying concepts in documents and queries.

Personalized retrieval: Alternative systems aim to provide personalized search results based on user preferences, search history, or user profiles. They may employ techniques like collaborative filtering or recommendation algorithms to tailor the results to individual users.

Multimedia retrieval: Alternative systems deal with retrieving multimedia content, such as images, audio, or video. These systems employ techniques like content-based image retrieval or speech recognition to match and retrieve multimedia data based on visual or acoustic features.

Cross-lingual retrieval: Alternative systems facilitate retrieval of information across different languages. They incorporate techniques like machine translation, cross-lingual information retrieval models, or language adaptation methods to bridge the language barrier and retrieve relevant information in the user's preferred language.

It's significant to note that these categories are not mutually exclusive, and modern information retrieval systems often combine multiple design features to provide more accurate and diverse search results.

6.1.1 Design structures of information retrieval (IR) systems

Let's explore the key design features of Information Retrieval (IR) systems:

Inverted index: The central data structure in most IR systems is the inverted index. This structure maintains a list for each word, detailing all the documents containing that word and the frequency of its occurrences in each document. This enables efficient querying for instances of a specific word.

Stop word elimination: Stop words refer to high-frequency words that are unlikely to significantly contribute to search results. These words, such as "a," "an," "the," and common prepositions like "in," "of," "for," and "at," carry less semantic weight. By creating a stop list and eliminating these words, the size of the inverted index can be reduced. However, caution must be exercised to avoid removing terms that are important for search queries.

Stemming: Stemming involves simplifying words by removing suffixes and other affixes to obtain their base forms. For instance, words like "laughing," "laughs," and "laughed" would be stemmed to the root word "laugh." This process aids in matching variations of a word and enhances retrieval accuracy.

Next, we will delve into important IR models. One of the earliest models is the Boolean model.

The Boolean model: This is the oldest IR model, rooted in set theory and Boolean algebra. In this model, documents are treated as sets of terms, and queries are expressed as Boolean expressions involving terms and logical operators such as AND, OR, and NOT. The Boolean Model encompasses these elements:

D: A set of terms representing indexing terms within a document, with each term marked as present (1) or absent (0).
Q: A Boolean expression comprising index terms and logical operators like AND, OR, and NOT.
F: A Boolean algebra framework applied to sets of terms and sets of documents.

Regarding relevance feedback in the Boolean IR model, the prediction of relevance can be defined as follows:

R: A document is predicted as relevant to the query expression if and only if it satisfies the query expression according to the formula:
((text OR information) AND relevant AND NOT theory).

In this model, a query term offers an unambiguous definition of a set of documents. For instance, a query with the term "economic" defines the set of documents indexed with the term "economic."

Combining terms using the Boolean AND operator produces a document set that is smaller or equal to the document sets of individual terms. For instance, a query combining "social" and "economic" produces a document set representing documents indexed with both terms, resulting in the intersection of these sets.

Combining terms using the Boolean OR operator yields a document set that is larger or equal to the document sets of individual terms. For instance, a query with terms "social" or "economic" produces a document set representing documents indexed with either "social" or "economic," resulting in the union of these sets.

6.2 Exploring Information Retrieval Models: Classical, Non-classical, Alternative

There are several models of information retrieval that have been proposed and used in the field. These models provide different approaches and perspectives on how information retrieval systems should function. Here are some of the prominent models:

1. Boolean model: The Boolean model is one of the initial and simplest models of information retrieval. It is based on Boolean logic and uses Boolean operators (AND, OR, NOT) to combine query terms and match them against documents. The model retrieves documents that exactly match the user's query.

2. Vector space model (VSM): The vector space model represents documents and queries as vectors in a high-dimensional space, where each dimension corresponds to a term. The similarity between a document and a query is calculated using measures such as cosine similarity. The VSM ranks documents based on their similarity to the query and retrieves the top-ranked documents.

3. Probabilistic models: Probabilistic models, such as the probabilistic relevance model (PRM) and the language model, estimation the probability of significance between a text and a query. These models consider the statistical properties of the document collection and the query to rank the documents based on their relevance probabilities.

4. Latent semantic indexing (LSI): LSI is a technique that applies singular value decomposition (SVD) to a term-document matrix to identify latent semantic relationships between terms and documents. It represents documents and queries in a lower-dimensional latent semantic space, allowing for capturing the underlying semantic meaning rather than relying solely on exact term matches.

5. Latent Dirichlet allocation (LDA): LDA is a topic model technique that represents documents as mixtures of topics. It assumes that documents are generated based on a spreading of topics, and each topic is a distribution of terms. LDA can be used to identify the most relevant topics to a query and retrieve documents associated with those topics.

6. Neural network models: With the advancement of deep learning, neural network models have been applied to information retrieval. Models like convolutional neural networks (CNNs) and recurrent neural networks (RNNs) have been used for text classification, document ranking, and query understanding tasks, improving the accuracy and effectiveness of retrieval systems.

7. Knowledge graph-based models: Knowledge graph-based models utilize structured knowledge graphs to enhance information retrieval. They leverage graph-based representations to capture relationships between entities, concepts, and attributes. These models enable semantic search, entity-based retrieval, and support for complex queries involving entity relationships.

8. Reinforcement learning-based models: Reinforcement learning-based models employ techniques from reinforcement learning to optimize the information retrieval process. These models learn from user interactions and feedback to improve the relevance of retrieved results over time.

It's significant to note that these models are not mutually exclusive, and many modern information retrieval systems combine multiple models or incorporate elements from various models to provide more accurate and effective retrieval capabilities.

When it comes to information retrieval, lexical resources show a vital role in enhancing the effectiveness and correctness of retrieval systems. Lexical resources refer to structured collections of words, terms, and their various properties, which are used to improve the retrieval process. Here are some models of information retrieval that utilize lexical resources for evaluation.

6.3 Understanding Lexical Resources

1. WordNet: WordNet is a broadly used lexical reserve that organizes words into synsets (sets of synonymous words) and provides semantic relationships between them. In information retrieval, WordNet is employed to expand queries by adding synonyms or related terms, thereby improving recall and addressing the issue of term mismatch between queries and documents.

2. Thesauri: Thesauri are collections of words and phrases that provide synonyms, antonyms, and related terms. They help in expanding queries by suggesting alternative terms that can be used to retrieve relevant documents. Thesauri-based models enable more comprehensive retrieval by considering various lexical variations and semantic relationships.

3. Ontologies: Ontologies are knowledge representations that define concepts, relationships, and properties within a specific domain. They capture hierarchical relationships, attributes, and semantic constraints. In information retrieval, ontologies can be used to enrich queries by leveraging domain-specific knowledge and enhancing the precision and relevance of the retrieved results.

4. Terminological resources: Terminological resources, such as controlled vocabularies and domain-specific dictionaries, provide standardized terms and their definitions within a specific field. They ensure consistent terminology usage and facilitate accurate retrieval by mapping user queries and document content to the appropriate terms in the domain.

5. Lexical normalization: Lexical normalization models aim to address variations in word forms and spelling. They use lexical resources to normalize terms by applying stemming, lemmatization, or morphological analysis. This normalization process helps to overcome variations in word usage and retrieve documents that match the underlying concept rather than exact word forms.

6. Lexical disambiguation: Lexical disambiguation models utilize lexical resources to resolve word sense ambiguity. Words often have multiple meanings, and disambiguation techniques use resources like WordNet or sense inventories to determine the most appropriate sense of a word in a specific context. This enhances the accuracy of retrieval by ensuring that the intended meaning of the query is considered.

7. Named entity recognition (NER): NER models classify and categorize named entities, such as names of people, organizations, locations, or specific terms, in text documents. Lexical resources, including gazetteers or lists of names and entities, assist in recognizing and disambiguating named entities in enquiries and documents, enabling more precise retrieval results.

These models demonstrate how lexical resources contribute to information retrieval by expanding queries, capturing semantic relationships, normalizing and disambiguating terms, and leveraging domain-specific knowledge. By incorporating lexical resources, retrieval systems can improve precision, recall, and relevance in retrieving the most pertinent information for users.

6.3.1 Introduction to Word Embeddings

Word embeddings are a general technique used in natural language processing (NLP) and information retrieval to represent words as numerical vectors. Word embeddings capture the semantic and contextual data of words in a dense and continuous vector space, enabling machines to understand and reason about words based on their relationships with other words. Here's an overview of word embeddings:

1. Representation of words: Word embeddings represent words as high-dimensional vectors in a continuous vector space. Each dimension in the vector represents a dissimilar aspect or feature of the word. For example, words with similar meanings or usage tend to have vectors that are close to each other in the vector space.

2. Distributional hypothesis: Word embeddings are built on the distributional hypothesis, which states that words that happen in similar contexts often have comparable meanings. By analyzing the co-occurrence patterns of words in large text corpora, word embeddings detention the semantic relations between words founded on their contextual usage.

3. Training methods: Word embeddings are typically learned through unsupervised learning methods, most commonly using neural network architectures. The training process involves presenting words or word sequences to the model, which then adjusts the word vectors based on the context in which the words appear. Popular algorithms for training word embeddings include Word2Vec, GloVe, and FastText.

4. Similarity and distance measures: Word embeddings allow for measuring the similarity or distance between words based on the regular properties of the vector space. Cosine similarity is commonly used to compute the similarity between word vectors. Words that are semantically similar tend to have higher cosine similarities, while dissimilar words have lower similarities.

5. Analogies and relationships: Word embeddings can capture various linguistic relationships and analogies. For example, by performing vector operations such as addition and subtraction, it is possible to find word vectors that represent analogies. For instance, "king − man + woman" would yield a vector that is close to the vector representation of "queen."

6. Pretrained word embeddings: Pretrained word embeddings are word vectors that have been trained on large corpora and made available for direct use. These embeddings capture general semantic information and can be beneficial in various NLP tasks, even when the specific domain or dataset is different from the original training data. Popular pretrained word embeddings include Word2Vec, GloVe, and BERT embeddings.

7. Applications: Word embeddings have been positively useful in a wide range of NLP tasks, including text classification, sentiment analysis, information retrieval, machine translation, question-answering systems, and more. They enable machines to understand and reason about words in a more meaningful and context-aware manner.

Word embeddings have revolutionized NLP and information retrieval by providing rich representations of words that capture their semantic properties. They have significantly improved the performance of various NLP tasks and are widely used in developing intelligent systems that work with human language [20].

6.3.2 Detailed insights into Word2Vec and GloVe

Word2Vec: Word2Vec is a general algorithm for knowledge word embeddings, which are dense vector representations of words in a continuous vector space. It was developed by Tomas Mikolov et al. at Google in 2013. Word2Vec is trained on large text corpora to capture the semantic and syntactic relationships between words. Here are the key aspects of Word2Vec:

1. **Training methods:** Word2Vec employs two main training methods: Continuous bag of words (CBOW) and Skip-gram.

   - **CBOW:** CBOW predicts the target word based on its surrounding context words. It takes a sequence of context words as input and predicts the target word at the center of the sequence. CBOW is faster to train and works well for frequently occurring words.
   - **Skip-gram:** Skip-gram, on the other hand, predicts the context words given the target word. It takes a target word as input and tries to predict the surrounding context words. Skip-gram is slower but performs better for infrequent or rare words.

2. **Neural network architecture:** Word2Vec employs a shallow neural network with a single hidden layer. The hidden layer represents the learned word embeddings. The input and output layers use one-hot encoding to represent words.

3. **Context window:** Word2Vec considers a fixed-size context window around each target word. The window size determines the number of context words taken into account during training. A larger window captures more global context, while a smaller window focuses on local context.

4. **Negative sampling:** To improve training efficiency, Word2Vec employs negative sampling. Instead of using all words in the vocabulary for training, negative sampling randomly selects a small number of negative examples (words that are not in the context) to update the word embeddings. This speeds up training and leads to more meaningful word representations.

5. **Word similarity and analogy:** Word2Vec embeddings enable measuring the similarity between words using cosine similarity. Words that are semantically similar have higher cosine similarities. Additionally, Word2Vec embeddings allow for finding analogies by performing vector operations such as addition and subtraction. For example, "king − man + woman" would yield a vector that is close to the vector representation of "queen."

6. **Pretrained word embeddings:** Word2Vec models can be trained on large-scale text corpora and pretrained word embeddings are widely available. These pretrained embeddings capture general semantic properties and can be used in various downstream NLP tasks, even with different domain-specific data.

Word2Vec has been widely adopted due to its effectiveness in capturing semantic relationships between words and its ability to generate high-quality word embeddings. It has been used in a wide range of applications, including information retrieval, text classification, named entity recognition, and machine translation, to name a few.

GloVe: GloVe (global vectors for word representation) is an unsupervised learning algorithm for obtaining word embeddings. Word embeddings are vector representations of words in a continuous vector space, where words with similar meanings or contexts are closer together.

GloVe was developed by researchers at Stanford University and is designed to capture both global co-occurrence statistics of words and local context information. It leverages the idea that word vectors can be represented as ratios of word co-occurrence probabilities.

Here are the key steps involved in training GloVe embeddings:

1. **Co-occurrence matrix:** The first step is to construct a co-occurrence matrix that captures the frequency of word co-occurrences in a large corpus of text. The matrix represents the global word-word co-occurrence statistics.

2. **Weighting:** The co-occurrence matrix is then transformed to give more importance to certain word pairs while down-weighting others. This is done to mitigate the impact of extremely frequent or rare word pairs.

3. **Training objective:** GloVe defines a training objective based on the idea that the ratio of co-occurrence probabilities of two words should be proportional to the ratio of their vector dot products. It aims to learn word vectors that satisfy this relationship.

4. **Optimization:** The objective function is optimized using techniques such as stochastic gradient descent to adjust the word vectors iteratively. The goal is to minimize the difference between the dot products of word vectors and the logarithm of the co-occurrence ratios.

5. **Word embeddings:** After training, the resulting word vectors capture semantic and syntactic relationships between words. Words with similar meanings or contexts are represented by vectors that are closer together in the vector space.

GloVe embeddings have been widely used in various natural language processing tasks, such as word similarity, text classification, machine translation, and information retrieval. They provide a dense representation of words that can capture fine-grained relationships and improve the performance of downstream NLP models.

Pre-trained GloVe embeddings are readily available for download, having been trained on extensive corpora such as Wikipedia and Common Crawl. These embeddings can be employed as initializations or directly integrated into NLP models to harness the benefits of learned word representations.

Distributional word representations, commonly referred to as word embeddings, are pervasive in modern NLP. Initial efforts focused on constructing representations for individual word types. Recent studies have highlighted that lemmatization and part-of-speech (POS) disambiguation of target words in isolation enhance the performance of word embeddings across a range of downstream tasks. However, the underlying reasons for these enhancements, the qualitative impacts of these operations, and the cumulative effects of combining lemmatized and POS-disambiguated targets have received less attention. This research aims to address these gaps and provide a comprehensive perspective on previous findings.

This study explores the impact of lemmatization and POS tagging on word embedding performance through a novel resource-based evaluation scenario, as well as established similarity benchmarks. The research demonstrates that lemmatization and POS tagging yield complementary qualitative and vocabulary-level effects, producing the most significant benefits when used in conjunction. The analysis reveals that the improvements are particularly pronounced for verbs, and the study showcases how lemmatization and POS tagging implicitly address issues specific to verbs. The observed enhancement is attributed to a better conceptual alignment between word embeddings and lexical resources, underscoring the importance of conceptually plausible modeling of word embedding targets.

Word2Vec, a technique in natural language processing, is designed to learn word associations. Employing neural network models, a trained Word2Vec model can identify synonyms, antonyms, and suggest words to complete incomplete sentences. The technique utilizes vectors to represent distinct words, and cosine similarity between vectors determines semantic similarity levels between words.

Word2Vec comprises a family of models and optimizers that facilitate the learning of word embeddings from large word corpora. Two primary methods are used for representing words:

- **Continuous bag of words (CBOW) method:** This approach predicts words that can complete a partially unfinished sentence based on surrounding context words. The context considered for prediction depends on words preceding and following the predicted word. These methods are termed bag-of-words methods as the word order in context is disregarded.
- **Skip-gram method:** This method predicts context or neighboring words given a current word within the same sentence. The Skip-gram model uses the input of each word in the corpus to predict context words using the embedding weights in the hidden or embedding layer.

The fundamental architectures of the CBOW and Skip-gram models are illustrated in Figure 6.2.

Figure 6.2: An overview of CBOW and Skip-gram models.

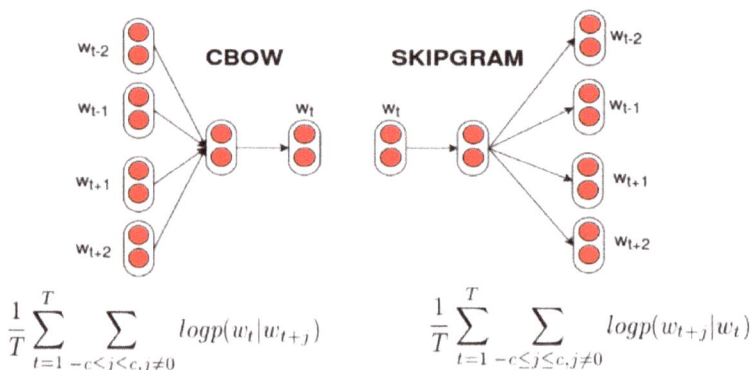

$$\frac{1}{T}\sum_{t=1}^{T}\sum_{-c\leq j\leq c, j\neq 0} logp(w_t|w_{t+j})$$

$$\frac{1}{T}\sum_{t=1}^{T}\sum_{-c\leq j\leq c, j\neq 0} logp(w_{t+j}|w_t)$$

GloVe, a portmanteau of "global" and "vectors," is a model employed for distributed word representation. It utilizes an unsupervised learning algorithm to convert words into vectorized forms. This algorithm maps words into a space where the semantic similarity between words is determined by the distance between their corresponding vectors. The core concept involves training a corpus using aggregated global word–word co-occurrence statistics. The outcome of this training provides a representation of the subspace in which the words of interest are situated. GloVe was initiated as an open-source project at Stanford University and was introduced in 2014.

Training procedure for the GloVe model: The GloVe model employs the matrix factorization technique for generating word embeddings based on the word-context matrix. The process commences by constructing a sizable matrix that captures the co-occurrence information of words. The matrix is structured to establish relationships between words through statistical analysis. The co-occurrence matrix furnishes insights into the occurrences of words in various pairs.

Refer to Figure 6.3 for further clarity.

Figure 6.3: Matrix factorization is used to embed words in the word–context matrix.

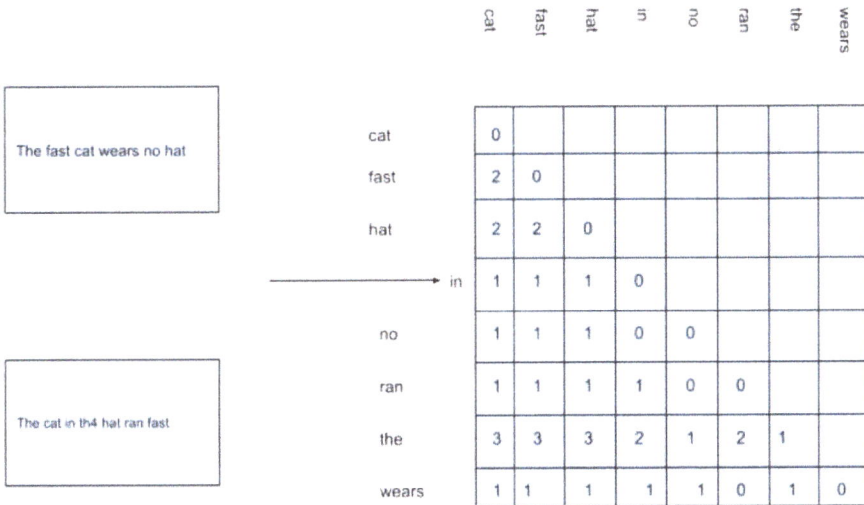

	cat	fast	hat	in	no	ran	the	wears
cat	0							
fast	2	0						
hat	2	2	0					
in	1	1	1	0				
no	1	1	1	0	0			
ran	1	1	1	1	0	0		
the	3	3	3	2	1	2	1	
wears	1	1	1	1	1	0	1	0

The fast cat wears no hat

The cat in th4 hat ran fast

In the provided image, a matrix has been constructed by considering the distinct words from two sentences presented on the left side. It's evident from the matrix that the word "the" appears three times in conjunction with "cat," "fast," and "hat," resulting in a value of 3 each time.

This matrix facilitates the computation of probability ratios between any two pairs of words. For instance, consider the probabilities of (cat/fast) = 1 and (cat/the) = 0.5. The ratio of these probabilities, in this case, would be 2. Utilizing this ratio, we can deduce that "fast" holds greater relevance than "the," based on the probabilities.

The GloVe method is represented mathematically through this approach.

$$F\left(w_i, w_j, \tilde{w}_k\right) = \frac{P_{ik}}{P_{jk}}$$

Let's compare Word2Vec and GloVe based on various parameters:

- **Training procedures:** Word2Vec is a predictive model trained to predict context words given a target word (Skip-gram method) or predict a target word given a context (CBOW method). It uses trainable embedding weights to map words to embeddings.

GloVe involves matrix factorization on the word–context matrix. Each word appears in various contexts in a large corpus, and matrix factorization reduces this high-dimensional matrix into a lower-dimensional one, resulting in vector representations for words.

- **Loss functions:** Word2Vec's loss function relates to the model's predictions, improving as accuracy increases, leading to better word embeddings.
  In GloVe, the goal is to minimize the reconstruction loss of the lower-dimensional matrix, capturing most of the variance in high-dimensional data.

- **Learning methods:** Word2Vec uses a three-layer neural network to generate word vectors and perform word pair classification. GloVe aims to use the co-occurrence matrix to learn linear relationships between words.

- **Generate output:** Word2Vec-generated embeddings can capture linear relationships between words, such as "king" − "man" + "woman" → "queen" or "better" − "good" + "bad" → "worse". GloVe initially struggled with such linear relationships but has improved in this aspect.

GloVe focuses on the weightage of word–word co-occurrence probabilities that encode meaning. Word2Vec works on maximizing co-occurrence probabilities to enhance accuracy.

- **Computation time:** Word2Vec often employs negative sampling, converting the softmax function into a sigmoid function. This results in cone-shaped clusters in the vector space, making Word2Vec computation faster. GloVe's vectors are more discrete in space.

- **Final thoughts:** In this section, we delved into Word2Vec and GloVe models, their applications, training procedures, and quick implementations using gensim. We compared these models based on various parameters, shedding light on their differences. This section provides insights into these popular word embedding techniques.

7

Unsupervised Methods in NLP

Significant advancements have taken place in the field of natural language processing (NLP) over the past few years. The landscape of NLP has undergone a profound transformation, with traditional approaches governed by rules and statistical models rapidly giving way to more robust methods rooted in machine learning, particularly deep learning.

Unsupervised machine learning, a notable approach, revolves around training models without the need for prior tagging or annotation. Several of these techniques are surprisingly straightforward to comprehend.

Clustering, for instance, involves the act of grouping similar documents into distinct sets or clusters. These clusters are subsequently organized based on their relevance and significance, often through hierarchical clustering.

Another form of unsupervised learning is latent semantic indexing (LSI). This method identifies recurring associations between words and phrases. LSI proves valuable in scenarios like faceted searches or generating search results that extend beyond the exact search term. For instance, a search for "manifold" may also yield results containing the term "exhaust," considering their close correlation in discussions about internal combustion engines.

Matrix factorization stands as another technique employed in unsupervised NLP machine learning. This technique employs "latent factors" to deconstruct a large matrix into a blend of two smaller matrices. These latent factors represent commonalities between items. Consider the sentence, "I threw the ball over the mountain." In this context, the term "threw" is more closely linked to "ball" than to "mountain." While humans intuitively grasp the factors contributing to something being throwable, an NLP algorithm necessitates training to discern such distinctions [24].

Unsupervised learning, although intricate, demands less effort and data compared to its supervised counterpart. At Lexalytics, we leverage unsupervised learning algorithms to establish a foundational grasp of language mechanics. By extracting vital patterns from extensive collections of text documents, we empower our models to comprehend the most plausible interpretations.

Unsupervised methods in natural language processing (NLP) refer to techniques and algorithms that do not require labeled data or explicit supervision during training. These methods aim to discover patterns, structures, and relationships within text data in an unsupervised manner. Here are some commonly used unsupervised methods in NLP:

1. Clustering: Clustering algorithms group similar documents or words together based on their characteristics. Techniques like K-means, hierarchical clustering, and DBSCAN are commonly used for unsupervised document clustering and word clustering tasks.

2. Topic modeling: Topic modeling algorithms aim to uncover latent topics or themes present in a collection of documents. Latent Dirichlet allocation (LDA) and non-negative matrix factorization (NMF) are popular unsupervised topic modeling algorithms. These methods identify the underlying topics by analyzing the co-occurrence patterns of words in the documents.

3. Word embeddings: Word embeddings represent words or phrases as dense vector representations in a continuous space. Models like Word2Vec, GloVe, and fastText use unsupervised learning to learn word embeddings. These embeddings capture semantic and syntactic associations between words, enabling various downstream NLP responsibilities such as word similarity, word analogy, and text sorting.

4. Word clustering: Unsupervised word clustering algorithms group words into clusters based on their semantic or syntactic similarities. These algorithms analyze word co-occurrence patterns in large text corpora to identify related words. Hierarchical clustering, K-means, and spectral clustering are commonly used methods for unsupervised word clustering.

5. Anomaly detection: Unsupervised anomaly detection methods identify unusual or outlier instances in a dataset. In NLP, these methods can be used to detect anomalous documents or sentences based on their linguistic character-istics, such as word frequency, sentence length, or grammatical structure. Tech-niques like One-Class SVM, Isolation Forest, and Autoencoders are commonly applied for anomaly detection in NLP.

6. Sentence embeddings: Similar to word embeddings, sentence embeddings represent entire sentences or paragraphs as dense vector representations. Mod-els like Doc2Vec, Universal Sentence Encoder, and BERT (via fine-tuning) can learn unsupervised sentence embeddings. These embeddings capture the semantic meaning and contextual information of sentences, facilitating tasks such as sentence similarity, sentiment analysis, and text classification.

These are just a few examples of unsupervised methods in NLP. Unsu-pervised learning techniques play a crucial role in discovering patterns and extracting useful information from large amounts of unannotated text data, enabling various NLP applications and downstream tasks.

7.1 Harnessing Graphical Models for Sequence Labeling

Graphical models are powerful tools for sequence labeling in natural language processing (NLP). They provide a probabilistic framework to model dependen-cies and capture contextual information between the elements of a sequence. Two commonly used graphical models for sequence labeling in NLP are hidden Markov models (HMMs) and conditional random fields (CRFs) [28].

1. Hidden Markov models (HMMs): HMMs are generative models that assume a hidden state sequence generates an observed sequence. In the context of NLP, the hidden states can represent the underlying labels or tags, while the observed sequence corresponds to the words or tokens in a sentence. HMMs capture the transition probabilities between states and emission probabilities for observations. They make the Markov assumption that the current hidden state depends only on the previous state.

HMMs are often used for tasks like part-of-speech tagging, where each word in a sentence is assigned a grammatical label. The Viterbi algorithm is commonly employed to find the most likely sequence of hidden states (tags) given the observed sequence (words).

Hidden Markov models (HMMs) are probabilistic graphical models widely used for sequential data modeling, including sequence labeling tasks in nat-ural language processing (NLP). HMMs are generative models that assume there is an underlying, unobserved sequence of hidden states that generate the observed sequence of symbols.

In the context of NLP sequence labeling, HMMs can be used to model the relationship between the sequence of words or characters (observations) and the corresponding sequence of labels (hidden states). The hidden states represent the labels or tags, such as part-of-speech tags or named entity labels, while the observations represent the words or characters in the text.

The key components of an HMM are:

- **Hidden states (labels):** These represent the labels or tags to be assigned to each element in the sequence. For example, in part-of-speech tagging, the hidden states could be nouns, verbs, adjectives, etc.
- **Observations:** These represent the observed sequence of elements in the text, such as words or characters.
- **Transition probabilities:** These capture the probability of transitioning from one hidden state to another. For example, in part-of-speech tagging, the transition probability could represent the likelihood of transitioning from a noun to a verb.
- **Emission probabilities:** These represent the probability of observing a specific element (word or character) given a hidden state (label). For example, in part-of-speech tagging, the emission probability could represent the likelihood of observing the word "cat" given the hidden state "noun".

During training, the parameters of the HMM, including the transition probabilities and emission probabilities, are estimated using maximum likelihood estimation or other statistical estimation techniques. The Viterbi algorithm or the forward-backward algorithm can be used to efficiently compute the most likely sequence of hidden states (labels) given the observed sequence.

HMMs have been widely used for various NLP tasks, including part-of-speech tagging, named entity recognition, speech recognition, and machine translation. While HMMs have been effective for modeling sequential dependencies, they make the simplifying assumption of the Markov property, which assumes that the current state depends only on the previous state. This assumption might not always hold in complex NLP scenarios, and more advanced models like Conditional Random Fields (CRFs) have been developed to overcome this limitation.

2. Conditional random fields (CRFs):

CRFs are discriminative models that model the conditional probability of a sequence given the observed features. In NLP, CRFs are widely used for tasks such as named entity recognition, chunking, and semantic role labeling. CRFs can capture dependencies between neighboring labels while considering the entire input sequence.

CRFs differ from HMMs in that they directly model the conditional distribution of the output sequence given the input sequence, rather than generating the output sequence from hidden states. CRFs can incorporate rich feature representations, including lexical, syntactic, and contextual features, to make more informed labeling decisions.

CRFs can be trained using maximum likelihood estimation or other optimization techniques, and the Viterbi algorithm is commonly used for decoding the most likely sequence of labels given the input sequence.

Both HMMs and CRFs have their strengths and weaknesses. HMMs are simpler and computationally efficient, but they make strong independence assumptions. CRFs are more flexible and can model complex feature interactions, but they can be more computationally expensive. The choice between the two depends on the specific task and the characteristics of the data. [26]

Overall, graphical models provide a probabilistic framework that leverages the dependencies between sequence elements, enabling more accurate and context-aware sequence labeling in NLP.

Conditional random fields (CRFs) are probabilistic graphical models that are commonly used for sequence labeling tasks in natural language processing (NLP). CRFs are discriminative models that model the conditional probability of a sequence of labels given an input sequence of observations.

CRFs extend hidden Markov models (HMMs) by relaxing the "Markov assumption" that the current state only depends on the previous state. CRFs allow for more complex dependencies between labels in the sequence, taking into account the entire input sequence during prediction. This makes CRFs particularly suitable for tasks where context plays a crucial role, such as part-of-speech tagging, named entity recognition, and chunking.

The main components of a CRF include:

- **Hidden states (labels):** These represent the labels or tags to be assigned to each element in the sequence. For example, in part-of-speech tagging, the hidden states could be noun, verb, adjective, etc.
- **Observations:** These represent the observed sequence of elements in the text, such as words or characters.
- **Feature functions:** CRFs define a set of feature functions that capture the relationship between the observed sequence and the hidden labels. Feature functions take into account both the current observation and the current and previous labels.

- **Parameters:** Each feature function is associated with a parameter that models the strength of the relationship between the observed sequence and the hidden labels.

During training, the parameters of the CRF are estimated using techniques like maximum likelihood estimation or regularized maximum likelihood estimation. The objective is to find the parameters that maximize the conditional likelihood of the true labels given the observed sequence.

During inference or prediction, CRFs use techniques like the Viterbi algorithm or belief propagation to find the most likely sequence of labels given the observed sequence. The CRF takes into account the dependencies between labels and jointly models the probability distribution over all possible label sequences.

CRFs have been widely used in various NLP tasks where sequential labeling is required. Compared to HMMs, CRFs offer more flexibility in modeling complex dependencies, leading to improved performance on tasks that involve rich contextual information.

8

Summary

This text is an introduction to natural language processing (NLP). It covers parsing, syntax, language modelling, smoothed estimation and language modelling, semantic analysis and discourse processing, natural language generation and machine translation, information retrieval and lexical resources, and unsupervised methods in NLP.

Natural language processing (NLP) is a subfield of artificial intelligence that aims to bridge the gap between human communication and machine understanding. It involves several key tasks, including language translation and sentiment analysis.

Text is preprocessed by removing punctuation, converting text to lowercase, and handling stop words. Part-of-speech tagging, named entity recognition, sentiment analysis, language modeling, and neural machine translation are used in machine translation systems.

NLP has many practical applications across industries, and is a rapidly growing area of research and development.

8.1 Introduction to NLP

Natural language processing (NLP) involves the development of algorithms and models to understand, interpret, and generate human language.

NLP enables computers to understand, analyze, and generate natural language text or speech. It involves several steps, including linguistics, statistical models, machine learning, and deep learning methods.

NLP involves cleaning and transforming raw text data, including tokenization, removing punctuation and stop words, normalizing text, and stemming. It also involves analyzing the structure and meaning of individual words, determining the relationships between words, and inferring the meaning of words and phrases in context.

8.2 Background and Overview

The field of natural language processing began in the 1940s, after World War II, when people hoped to create a machine that could do translation automatically. However, some researchers found issues with the development of NLP, including Noam Chomsky.

Researchers split into two divisions concerning NLP around 1957: symbolic and stochastic. Symbolic researchers focused on formal languages and generating syntax, while stochastic researchers worked on optical character recognition.

Natural language processing (NLP) helps computers understand, interpret, and utilize human languages. It also allows computers to read text, hear speech, and interpret it.

Content categorization, topic discovery and modeling, contextual extraction, sentiment analysis, text-to-speech and speech-to-text conversion, document summarization, and machine translation are all used to analyze large amounts of text.

8.3 Applications of NLP

NLP techniques are used in several applications, including sentiment analysis, language translation, information extraction, and question answering. These systems are used in chatbots, virtual assistants, and search engines to provide quick and accurate responses to user queries.

NLP techniques are used in text summarization, chatbots, virtual assistants, speech recognition, text classification, information retrieval, healthcare, and dictation software to understand and respond to user queries, provide interactive conversational experiences, and improve the user search experience.

Language serves as an instinctive medium to convey information and meaning, employing semantic cues such as words, signs, and images. The rising prominence of machine learning and artificial intelligence has ignited a surge of interest, with natural language processing (NLP) poised to reach heightened levels of sophistication.

Among the initial and fundamental applications of NLP online, email filters stand out. Gmail's email classification system, for instance, harnesses NLP to maintain an organized inbox by identifying important and relevant emails, ensuring prompt attention and response.

The realm of smart assistants, exemplified by Apple's Siri and Amazon's Alexa, revolves around recognizing speech patterns and furnishing context-driven responses. These assistants hold the promise of enriching our daily lives, simplifying tasks like making purchases, and even eliciting amusement through humorous interactions or answering queries about themselves.

NLP's influence extends to search engines as well, where the emphasis has shifted from exact search words to anticipating user intent. Search engines employ NLP to predict user inputs and furnish pertinent results based on similar search behaviors.

The prevalence of features like autocorrect, autocomplete, and predictive text on smartphones showcases NLP in action. These features progressively learn from user interactions, leading to intriguing experiments where entire sentences are composed solely using predictive text suggestions.

The evolution of language translation through NLP is remarkable, as tools can now discern the language from input text and provide accurate translations.

Corporate adoption of NLP is evident in the automation of phone interactions, where systems respond to customer queries with relevant information and even facilitate appointments such as scheduling oil changes or haircuts.

Incorporating natural language capabilities into data analysis workflows marks another development. This integration enables individuals to explore data using natural language queries or fragments, democratizing analytics within organizations.

Text analytics leverages an array of linguistic, statistical, and machine-learning techniques to dissect unstructured text data. This practice proves invaluable for gauging marketing campaign effectiveness, preemptively addressing trending customer concerns, and enhancing customer experiences through responsive service improvements.

8.4 Challenges of NLP Ambiguity

Ambiguity presents a formidable hurdle within the realm of natural language processing (NLP). The ever-shifting meanings of words, along with their context-dependent interpretations in diverse domains, contribute to this challenge.

Metonymy, for instance, introduces a layer of complexity. When we express that "Samsung is screaming for new management," we are not implying that the company is literally emitting vocalizations. Instead, this usage employs metonymy to convey a broader concept.

Metaphors further compound this complexity. They function to convey meanings beyond literal interpretations and often draw upon historical or fictional references. Managing metaphors proves particularly intricate due to their layered nature.

The prevalence of ambiguity underscores the considerable difficulty inherent in NLP, given the intricacies and subtleties of human language. Expert.ai addresses this challenge by offering solutions that effectively navigate ambiguity, resulting in heightened accuracy when grappling with the nuanced meanings of words.

Word sense disambiguation involves determining the correct meaning of a word in a given context, using pre-existing lexical resources like WordNet.

NLP applications can use user feedback to resolve ambiguity and improve their future responses. Complete disambiguation is not always possible, but these techniques can significantly improve the accuracy of language understanding and processing.

Term frequency-inverse document frequency (TF-IDF) is a statistical number that replicates the importance of a word in a document collection.

Transformer models have revolutionized NLP by capturing contextual information and achieving state-of-the-art results across several tasks.

8.5 Algorithms and Models in NLP

Natural language processing (NLP) includes many algorithms and models that are used for tasks like machine translation and text summarization. These models are often based on encoder-decoder architectures and can take variable-length input sequences and produce variable-length output sequences.

Machine translation, grammar and spell checking, text classification, named-entity recognition, summarization, text generation, topic modeling are the main tasks assigned to the developers of NLP technologies.

Lemmatization and stemming are two techniques that play a pivotal role in advancing natural language processing tasks. They facilitate the reduction of a word's various forms to a singular root, thereby diminishing the necessary data space and enhancing the potency and robustness of NLP algorithms.

Topic modeling constitutes a distinctive facet of natural language processing, aiming to identify overarching thematic concepts that can define a collection of texts. Latent Dirichlet allocation stands as a prominent method within NLP for achieving topic modeling.

Central to natural language processing, keyword extraction holds significant importance. Within this domain, a range of keyword extraction algorithms exist. Some focus solely on extracting individual words, while others encompass both words and phrases. Certain algorithms derive keywords by considering the entirety of the textual content.

In essence, these techniques and methods collectively contribute to the advancement of natural language processing by refining text analysis, thematic identification, and information extraction processes.

Knowledge graphs consist of three components: a subject, a predicate, and an entity. These components form a method for organizing information using triples. The popularity of knowledge graphs has grown notably in recent times.

A word cloud is a data visualization technique that arranges words from a text into a visual representation, with more significant terms displayed in larger fonts within a table.

Named entity recognition (NER) is a method in natural language processing that involves identifying potential candidates for NER algorithms and assigning them to predefined categories within the text.

Sentiment analysis ranks among the most frequently employed NLP techniques. It serves to interpret consumer surveys, ratings, and discussions on social media platforms. The naïve Bayes model is commonly utilized for sentiment analysis.

Text summarization, a domain within NLP, encompasses two main methods: extraction and abstraction. Extraction techniques create summaries by selecting key information, while abstraction methods generate summaries by composing new text that captures the essence of the original content.

The bag of words technique represents text as a collection of words, generating an incidence matrix that helps analyze and understand the textual content.

This strategy works better with some languages than others, especially tonal languages like Mandarin.

8.6 Knowledge Bottlenecks in NLP

Humans understand sentences like "I ran to the store because we ran out of milk" and "The house is looking really run down" easily.

Synonyms are words that convey the same idea but may have different levels of complexity. For building NLP systems, it's important to include all possible meanings and all possible synonyms.

Sarcasm involves using irony to mock, ridicule, or convey contempt. NLP systems have made progress in detecting and understanding sarcasm, but it remains an ongoing research challenge due to the subtleties and subjectivity involved.

Lexical ambiguity, semantic ambiguity, and syntactic ambiguity are all problems that can cause confusion in NLP. POS tagging is one NLP solution that can help solve the problem, somewhat.

Colloquialisms, slang, and culture-specific expressions pose significant challenges for NLP, especially when developing models intended for widespread application. Employing custom models that are regularly trained and updated can offer a viable solution to mitigate these issues.

Various businesses and industries utilize domain-specific languages, leading to the development of analysis tools tailored to these distinct fields, thereby enhancing accuracy and relevance.

AI and machine learning applications in NLP have predominantly focused on the most commonly used languages. However, many languages remain overlooked and underrepresented in processing efforts. Nevertheless, emerging techniques strive to identify and leverage universal linguistic similarities that transcend individual languages.

Machine learning's hunger for extensive data is well-known, and ongoing advancements in techniques continue to address this demand. While this evolution may introduce new challenges, continued research and development hold the potential to yield solutions in the near future.

SaaS text analysis platforms like Monkey Learn present users with the opportunity to train their own machine learning NLP models. This capability serves to alleviate several limitations associated with NLP processing, fostering increased flexibility and adaptability.

8.7 Introduction to Natural Language Toolkit (NLTK)

NLTK stands as a potent resource within the realm of natural language processing when utilizing Python. It aids in the transformation of text into numerical formats compatible with models.

Renowned for its capabilities in natural language processing (NLP), NLTK serves as a widely used Python library encompassing an array of tasks. These tasks encompass text preprocessing, tokenization, part-of-speech tagging, named entity recognition, sentiment analysis, and beyond.

Boasting a robust array of tools and resources, NLTK offers a comprehensive toolkit catering to both newcomers and seasoned researchers involved in various NLP endeavors. It is an indispensable asset for individuals at all levels of expertise

8.8 Case Study

Natural language processing (NLP) techniques can be applied to perform sentiment analysis on product reviews.

The company has gathered thousands of customer reviews for their products. The reviews are categorized into positive, negative, and neutral.

Machine learning models can be trained using labeled reviews and evaluated using metrics such as accuracy, precision, recall, and F1 score.

This case study demonstrates how NLP techniques can be applied to perform sentiment analysis on product reviews.

Parsing and syntax: Parsing is the process of analyzing a string of symbols according to the rules of a formal grammar. It is often performed as a method of understanding the exact meaning of a sentence or word.

Within computational linguistics, parsing refers to the formal analysis by a computer of a sentence or other string of words into its constituents.

The term is also used in psycholinguistics to describe language comprehension, and is especially common when discussing garden-path sentences.

Word-level analysis: Word-level analysis is an essential task in natural language processing, where the focus is on understanding and extracting meaningful information from individual words in a given text.

Stemming reduces words to their base form by removing prefixes and suffixes. It may result in non-dictionary words, unlike lemmatization.

Researchers and practitioners employ word-level analysis techniques to build robust models and applications capable of understanding human language.

Utilizing regular expressions: Regular expressions are supported in many programming languages and text editors, and are widely used for text search and replacement, data validation, parsing, and text preprocessing.

A regular expression is a language for searching for text using a specialized syntax.

Stephen Cole Kleene formalized the Regular Expression language, which is an algebraic notation for characterizing a set of strings.

"·" is a regular expression that indicates that the language contains an empty string. - X, Y, X.Y, X+Y, X*, and Y* are also regular expressions.

Normalization of text: Case normalization applies to languages that use uppercase and lowercase letters. It is helpful in semantic use cases, but may hinder performance in other cases.

Another common normalization step removes punctuation in the text. This may or may not be useful given the problem at hand.

Text normalization involves applying a series of rules and techniques to raw text data to improve accuracy, reduce noise, and ensure better understanding and processing of the text.

Text normalization is performed as a pre-processing step before feeding the text into models or algorithms.

Edit distance computation: The edit distance, also known as the Levenshtein distance, between two character strings represents the smallest count of edit operations needed to transform one string into the other. This metric finds utility in assigning varying weights to different edit operations based on the likelihood of letter substitutions.

The calculation of the edit distance between two strings entails determining the minimum number of operations essential to convert one string into the other.

The edit distance stands as a quantification of the dissimilarity between two character strings. It is defined as the smallest number of operations required for the transformation of one string into the other.

When the characters being compared are identical, the result is 1; otherwise, it's the minimum value among (M[i−1, j], M[i, j−1], M[i−1, j−1]) + 1.

Parsing and syntax-spelling relations: A natural language parser is a program that separates a series of text into smaller pieces based on the grammar rules.

A parser works by splitting a sequence of text into a bunch of words that are related in a sort of phrase. It is based on the structure of words and not on the context.

Parsing is the process of analyzing a sentence's grammatical structure to determine its syntactic components and their relationships, while syntax refers to the rules and principles that govern the arrangement of words and phrases to create grammatically correct sentences.

In natural language processing (NLP) or computational linguistics, spelling correction involves identifying and correcting misspelled words in text. Language models can be used to suggest corrections based on the context of the surrounding words.

Error detection and correction: Grammatical error correction (GEC) is the task of correcting different kinds of errors in text.

Spell checking is a language tool that flags misspelled/unintended words in the given text. It is categorized as "non-word errors" and "real-word errors".

Error detection and correction in natural language processing involves identifying and rectifying errors in text.

To achieve better accuracy and coverage in error detection and correction tasks, different techniques are often employed.

8.9 Words and their Classes

Modern grammars recognize four major word classes and five minor word classes, making nine total.

In natural language processing, words are identified by tokenization, which is the process of splitting text into individual words.

Interjections are words or phrases used to express emotions, surprise, or strong reactions. They are used in NLP techniques such as text generation, information extraction, and sentiment analysis.

8.10 Part of Speech Tagging

A part-of-speech tag signifies whether a word is a noun, adjective, verb, and so on.

The process of assigning one of the parts of speech to a given word is generally called part-of-speech (PoS) tagging. It falls under rule base POS tagging, stochastic POS tagging and transformation based tagging.

Part-of-speech tagging is a fundamental task in natural language processing (NLP) that helps in understanding the syntactic structure of a sentence.

8.11 Sentiment Classification with Naïve Bayes: Case Study

Naïve Bayes classification is a simple and powerful classification task in machine learning, and is used for textual data analysis.

Simple Bayes modolo arc othei names for naïve Bayes models, which apply Bayes' theorem to machine learning.

Step 1: Convert the text reviews into numerical feature vectors. Apply techniques like TF-IDF to assign weights to the words.

Step 2: Train a Naïve Bayes classifier using the training data.

Step 3: Use the trained Naïve Bayes classifier to classify new, unseen customer reviews.

Step 4: Use the trained Naïve Bayes classifier to classify new, unseen customer reviews.

In this case study, we built a sentiment classifier using Naïve Bayes for customer reviews.

Naïve Bayes is a classification algorithm that is commonly used in natural language processing (NLP) for tasks such as sentiment classification.

We will use the IMDb dataset to train and test our model, which contains 50,000 movie reviews.

We will use the Count Vectorizer class from the scikit-learn library to perform the preprocessing step.

After training the classifier, we will test it on the testing data and evaluate its performance using metrics such as accuracy, precision, and recall.

We can evaluate the performance of a classifier by looking at metrics such as accuracy, precision, and recall.

In this case study, we have used the Naïve Bayes algorithm to perform sentiment classification on movie reviews.

8.12 Smoothed Estimation and Language Modelling

To keep a language model from assigning zero probability to unseen events, we have to shave off a bit of probability mass from more frequent events and give it to the events we have never seen. This is called smoothing.

Smoothing techniques in natural language processing are used to determine the probability of any sequence of words occurring together when one or more words individually (unigram) or N-grams (bigram) in the given set have never occurred in the past.

Language modeling can be done statistically or neurally. Neural network methods achieve better results than classical methods on challenging tasks like speech recognition and machine translation.

8.13 N-gram Language Models: Understanding N-grams

A good N-gram language model can predict the next word in a sentence, i.e., the value of p(w|h). One way to estimate this probability is from relative frequency counts.

N-gram language models are used in natural language processing tasks such as language modeling, machine translation, speech recognition, and text generation.

To estimate the probability of a word given the previous two words, divide the count of the 3-gram by the count of the 2-gram.

8.14 Assessing Language Models: Evaluation Strategies

For language models, we can define accuracy in several ways, but the most straightforward way is to use the likelihood of the model with respect to the development or test data. The log likelihood is also commonly used, but it can cause numerical precision problems.

To evaluate a language model, you have to embed it in an application and measure how much the application improves. Unfortunately, this is very expensive, so you need an intrinsic evaluation metric.

For an intrinsic evaluation of a language model, we need a test set. This is done by measuring the model's performance on some unseen data.

Language model accuracy is measured by the perplexity, which is the exponent of the average negative log likelihood per word. The higher the perplexity, the more accurate the language model is.

Perplexity is a metric for evaluating language models that measures how well a model predicts a given text. Lower perplexity indicates better performance.

The F1 score is used to evaluate models in text classification, named entity recognition, and sentiment analysis. It is the harmonic mean of precision and recall.

In some cases, human evaluation is conducted to assess the quality of language models. This approach can provide valuable insights but is resource-intensive.

8.15 Challenges in Language Modelling

Language modeling in NLP is the task of predicting the next word or sequence of words in a given context. It is often used in machine translation, speech recognition, text generation, and sentiment analysis.

Language models use N-grams to estimate the probability of the next word given the previous n − 1 words in a training corpus.

Language models are trained on large datasets using techniques like maximum likelihood estimation or masked language modeling.

Once trained, language models can be used for many tasks, such as predicting the next word given a context, generating text from scratch, completing partial sentences, or evaluating the likelihood of a sentence.

Language modeling is a fundamental problem in natural language processing (NLP), and a good language model should be able to capture the syntax and semantics of a language and produce coherent and grammatically correct sentences.

There are different approaches to building language models, including N-gram models, recurrent neural network models, and transformer models. Transformer models use attention mechanisms and large amounts of data for training.

Language modeling is a fundamental problem in natural language processing (NLP) and involves capturing the statistical properties and patterns of language. It is the basis for various applications such as machine translation, speech recognition, text generation, and many others.

Language models such as recurrent neural networks, long short-term memory (LSTM) networks, and transformer models are based on deep learning and neural networks, and can generate coherent and contextually appropriate text.

Language modeling is a crucial task in NLP that enables models to generate, understand, and manipulate natural language text.

Language models are trained on large amounts of text data, but it is not possible to include all possible sentences and word combinations in the training data. Therefore, language models need to generalize well.

Generalization in language modeling can be challenging due to the presence of rare or infrequent words. Sub-word tokenization and character-level modeling can help mitigate this problem.

Language models need to understand different sentence structures, word placements, and semantic variations in order to generate coherent text.

Language models often rely on statistical techniques like smoothing or backoff methods to handle unknown words, while sub-word tokenization can help handle unknown words by breaking down words into smaller units that are more likely to be seen during training.

Generalization is a crucial aspect of language modeling that ensures the model's robustness and effectiveness in generating text.

The bigram denied the occurs a sufficient number of times in the WSJ Treebank3 corpus, but some perfectly acceptable English word sequences are bound to be missing from it.

Zeros in the training set hurt the performance of any application we want to run on this data. Furthermore, if some words have zero probability, we can't compute perplexity at all.

In a closed vocabulary system, the test set can only contain words from this lexicon, and there will be no unknown words. This is a reasonable assumption in some domains, such as speech recognition or machine translation.

In other cases, we have to deal with words we haven't seen before, and we model these potential unknown words by adding a pseudo-word called UNK>.

There are two common ways to train the probabilities of an unknown word model: (1) choose a fixed vocabulary in advance, (2) convert any OOV word to an unknown word token, (3) estimate the probabilities.

Handling unknown words in language modeling is important because encountering them during text generation or prediction can lead to incorrect or nonsensical outputs.

One common technique is to introduce a special token, often denoted as <UNK> to represent unknown words. This allows the model to learn a representation for unknown words.

Language models can be trained to generate sentences based on unknown words by breaking down the words into smaller sub-word units, by analyzing the morphological structure of the words, by using external resources, or by considering the context and syntactic structure of the sentence.

Language models have to be able to generate coherent and contextually appropriate text even when faced with unknown words.

Semantic analysis and discourse processing: Semantic analysis strives to comprehend the significance of natural language within the context of logical sentence structuring, grammar roles, and contextual cues.

In the realm of artificial intelligence, natural language processing stands as one of the most intricate challenges, with discourse processing emerging as a significant hurdle. This entails the construction of theories and models that elucidate the intricate interconnection of utterances to forge coherent discourse.

Semantic analysis involves mapping words and phrases to their corresponding semantic representations in order to capture the underlying meaning of the text.

Named entity recognition (NER) helps in understanding the key entities mentioned in the text by identifying and classifying named entities, word sense disambiguation (WSD), semantic role labeling (SRL), and sentiment analysis (SA).

Discourse processing involves understanding how sentences and utterances are connected and organized to form coherent and meaningful texts or conversations.

Discourse parsing involves identifying discourse segments, discourse relations, and discourse connectives, coreference resolution involves resolving references to entities or events across multiple sentences or utterances, and text coherence and cohesion involves examining the relationships between sentences or discourse units.

8.16 Semantic Analysis: Representing Meaning

Semantic analysis involves extracting meaning from text through the examination of its grammatical structure and the identification of connections among individual words.

Semantic analysis in natural language processing involves the task of representing the meaning of text in a structured and formal manner.

Distributional semantics is based on the idea that words with similar distributions in the text tend to have similar meanings. Logical formalisms and frame semantics provide formal languages for representing the meaning of sentences. Dependency-based representations model the syntactic structure of sentences using dependency relationships between words.

Different approaches to meaning representation in NLP are used in practical systems, and the choice depends on the specific task at hand.

8.17 Exploring Lexical Semantics

Lexical semantics constitutes the initial phase of semantic analysis, delving into the exploration of the meanings attributed to individual words. This encompassing field not only encompasses words but also extends its inquiry to sub-words, affixes (sub-units), compound words, and phrases.

Lexical semantics is a subfield of natural language processing that deals with the meaning of individual words and their relationships.

Lexical semantics deals with determining the correct sense of a word in a given context, using lexical resources, and measuring the semantic similarity between words. These techniques are used in NLP applications like machine translation, information retrieval, and automatic summarization. Lexical semantics explores the relationships between words and helps in building more accurate models for various NLP tasks. Lexical acquisition techniques contribute to improving the coverage and accuracy of lexical semantics in NLP systems.

8.18 Navigating Ambiguity

Ambiguity is a common challenge in natural language processing due to the inherent complexity and richness of human language. Ambiguity poses difficulties in understanding and processing language accurately.

Lexical ambiguity occurs when a word has multiple meanings, syntactic ambiguity occurs when a sentence can be parsed in multiple ways, and semantic ambiguity occurs when a sentence can be interpreted in multiple ways due to its underlying meaning.

Using contextual information, statistical methods, machine learning, and knowledge resources, we can disambiguate ambiguous language and infer the intended meaning.

Advances in techniques like deep learning, contextual embeddings, and pre-training models have shown promising results in improving disambiguation accuracy.

8.19 Resolving Word Sense Ambiguity

Word sense disambiguation stands as an initial challenge encountered by most NLP systems. Although part-of-speech taggers with exceptional accuracy can address the syntactic ambiguity of words, grappling with semantic ambiguity proves to be more intricate.

In the realm of natural language processing (NLP), word sense disambiguation assumes a pivotal role by striving to ascertain the accurate meaning of a word within a provided context.

Word sense disambiguation (WSD) relies on a sense inventory, context information, and supervised or unsupervised learning methods to disambiguate the meaning of words. Supervised approaches use annotated training data, while unsupervised approaches use statistical or clustering techniques to identify patterns in word usage and group similar contexts together.

Knowledge-based WSD methods use lexical resources and linguistic knowledge to determine the most appropriate sense for a given word.

WSD models can be trained using labeled data and the Lesk algorithm, supervised classification models, or word embeddings to estimate the similarity between word contexts and possible senses.

WSD is used in various NLP tasks such as machine translation, information retrieval, question answering, and text summarization. However, WSD remains a challenging task.

8.20 Discourse Processing: Cohesion in Text

Discourse processing involves analyzing the structure, coherence, and cohesion of texts or conversations. Cohesion refers to the ways in which various linguistic elements within a discourse are connected.

Reference, ellipsis, conjunctions and connectives contribute to the cohesion of a text by avoiding repetition and maintaining textual cohesion by indicating logical connections, contrasts, cause-effect relationships or temporal sequences. Repetition, synonyms, antonyms, and hyponyms can all contribute to lexical cohesion, and parallelism can enhance the flow and coherence of a text by creating a sense of symmetry or balance.

NLP systems use cohesive devices to improve the coherence and understandability of generated texts.

Cohesion is the relationship between grammatical and lexical elements in a text and can be created in many different ways, including reference, ellipsis, substitution, lexical cohesion and conjunction.

There are two referential devices that can create cohesion: anaphoric and cataphoric references. Anaphoric references refer back to someone or something that has been previously identified, while cataphoric references refer forward.

Exophoric reference refers to generics or abstracts without ever identifying them, while homophoric reference refers to specific entities through knowledge of their context.

8.21 Achieving Reference Resolution

To interpret a sentence, we need to know who or what entity is being talked about. Reference resolution is the task of determining what entities are referred to by which linguistic expression.

Coreference resolution is the task of finding referring expressions in a text that refer to the same entity.

The main problem with coreference resolution in English is the pronoun "it", because it has many uses.

Reference resolution involves identifying and connecting referring expressions to the entities they refer to in a given context, enabling accurate understanding and interpretation of language.

Pronouns refer to previously mentioned entities. Resolving pronouns correctly is essential for maintaining coherence and understanding in a discourse.

Resolving definite noun phrases involves identifying the correct referents based on context and shared knowledge.

Coreference resolution is the task of connecting multiple referring expressions within a discourse to the same entity. It plays a crucial role in understanding the relationships between entities and establishing coherence in a text.

Anaphoric expressions refer back to something mentioned earlier in the discourse. They can be pronouns, definite noun phrases, or other referring expressions.

Reference resolution is a challenging task in NLP that uses rule-based approaches, machine learning models, and deep learning methods.

8.22 Establishing Discourse Coherence and Structure

Coherence is used to evaluate the output quality of natural language generation systems. A coherent discourse must possess the following properties.

Discourse segmentation determines the types of structures for large discourse and is very significant for information retrieval, text summarization and information extraction kind of applications.

Discourse coherence and structure are important in natural language processing because they ensure that the different parts of a discourse are connected.

Discourse coherence is the overall clarity and logical connection of ideas within a discourse.

Coherence relations, discourse markers, textual cohesion, and discourse structure are all important in building coherent and well-structured language models. They help in understanding the intended meaning and organizing the discourse, as well as determining the relationships between different parts of the discourse.

Researchers in NLP have developed various techniques and models to analyze and generate coherent discourse, including discourse parsers, coherence modeling, and deep learning architectures.

8.23 Natural Language Generation and Machine Translation

8.23.1 Natural language generation: System architecture and applications

NLG software can be used to produce news and other time-sensitive stories on the internet.

NLG and MT are two important areas of natural language processing (NLP) that involve generating human-like text in different contexts.

Natural language generation (NLG) is the process of automatically generating human-like text or speech from structured data or other non-linguistic representations.

Machine translation (MT) involves the automatic translation of text from one language to another.

MT systems use linguistic rules and dictionaries to translate text, while NMT systems use neural networks to learn the mapping between source and target language sequences. Both NLG and MT are active research areas, with ongoing advancements in deep learning, large-scale language models, and multilingual representations.

8.23.2 Applications of NLG

Natural language generation (NLG) is a sub-field of natural language processing (NLP) that generates images or narratives in natural language from structured data. NLG often works closely with natural language understanding (NLU), another sub-field of NLP.

Content determination and text planning involves selecting information from a knowledge base, structuring the information into sentences and paragraphs, planning for a flowing narrative, and generating individual sentences in a grammatically correct manner.

Sentence planning involves determining the sentence structure, word order, and syntactic transformations, and takes the structured data from the content planning phase.

Referring expression generation considers the discourse context, the salience of different entities, and the conventions of reference in the target language.

NLG enables chatbots and virtual assistants to generate contextually relevant, informative, and engaging responses, as well as personalized recommendations, reports, and content for news articles, weather reports, sports summaries, or other forms of informational content.

NLG is used in chatbots and voice assistants, and to generate thousands of corporate earnings reports in seconds. It was used by BBC News to publish 689 local stories of 100K words in 10 hours.

Natural language reporting is used by businesses in a variety of industries to generate reports. These reports can help business leaders quickly reach conclusions and make good decisions.

Natural language generation (NLG) is a technology that uses artificial intelligence to generate natural language text, which is then processed by a human being.

NLG systems can automatically generate reports based on structured data, which are useful in fields such as finance, business analytics, and data-driven industries.

NLG enables chatbots and virtual assistants to generate human-like responses, and assist users with various tasks.

NLG systems can generate news stories from data sources, such as financial news, sports updates, and weather reports.

NLG can be used to interpret and communicate insights from complex data analytics, making it easier for decision-makers to understand and act upon the findings.

8.24 Machine Translation: Challenges and Approaches

Language is inherently ambiguous, and machine translation systems often struggle to resolve ambiguities accurately, leading to potential errors in translations.

MT systems often encounter rare or unseen words, which can lead to incorrect translations or the use of generic placeholders.

MT systems must handle morphological variations accurately to generate grammatically correct translations. However, errors can occur, especially in agglutinative languages.

Syntax and word order can be difficult to translate, leading to unnatural or ungrammatical translations.

MT systems may struggle to capture cultural and contextual nuances, leading to translations that lack cultural appropriateness.

Machine translation researchers are exploring approaches such as neural machine translation, transfer learning, domain adaptation, and leveraging large-scale multilingual models to improve translation quality.

8.24.1 Issues in machine translation

Machine translation software offers the convenience of swiftly translating entire documents with a single click. However, certain challenges persist that necessitate the involvement of a human translator.

The quality of machine translation is perpetually hindered due to its inability to comprehend the contextual nuances of language usage. The comprehension of linguistic context remains a forte of human understanding, eluding machine translation capabilities.

Apple's Siri, for instance, lacks autonomous reasoning abilities and consequently cannot provide feedback or engage in collaborative efforts. For crucial tasks like translating essential marketing content into foreign languages for a marketing team, direct collaboration with a professional translation organization becomes imperative.

While machine translation can proficiently handle certain subjects, it falls short of mastering the intricacies of language, which inherently involves substantial creativity. Human translators possess the capacity to infuse creativity into the subject matter, enhancing its expressiveness.

Machine translation's inadequacy in accounting for cultural values and norms can lead to unintended consequences such as miscommunicating with business partners or customers, or inadvertently causing offense.

The role of a human translator extends to ensuring consistency in terminology throughout a project, preventing reader confusion.

In essence, machine translation streamlines certain tasks but remains unable to replicate the nuanced context, cultural sensitivity, and creative intricacies that human translators effortlessly provide.

Machine translation systems often struggle to resolve ambiguities in translations due to lexical ambiguity, syntactic ambiguity, and semantic ambiguity.

MT systems often encounter rare or unseen words, which can lead to incorrect translations or the use of generic placeholders.

Languages exhibit rich morphological variations, and MT systems need to handle these variations accurately to generate grammatically correct translations.

The correct word order is a major challenge in machine translation.

MT systems may struggle to capture cultural and contextual nuances, leading to translations that lack cultural appropriateness.

Researchers are exploring approaches to improve machine translation quality, such as neural machine translation, transfer learning, domain adaptation, and leveraging large-scale multilingual models.

8.24.2 Diverse approaches to machine translation

Rule-based machine translation (RBMT) utilizes linguistic rules and dictionaries to translate text from the source language to the target language. It can be labor-intensive and may struggle with capturing language variations.

Statistical machine translation uses statistical models to translate text based on patterns and relationships between source and target language text. SMT systems require large amounts of parallel data for training and often rely on statistical algorithms for decoding.

Neural machine translation (NMT) uses artificial neural networks to translate text between source and target languages. It produces fluent translations and has shown significant improvements in translation accuracy.

Hybrid approaches combine different MT techniques to achieve better translation quality by combining their advantages.

Transfer learning and pre-trained models have gained popularity in machine translation, and can be used as a starting point for training MT systems. These models can generalize across languages and tasks, reducing the need for extensive language-specific training data.

Machine translation algorithms can be categorized based on their underlying principles. Rule-based approaches involve direct word-by-word translation, whereas corpus-based methods employ statistical probabilities to select the most likely translation from various options.

Rule-based machine translation (RBMT) relies on morphological, syntactic, and semantic analyses of both source and target languages. In contrast, corpus-based machine translation (CBMT) is built on the analysis of bilingual text collections.

Methods like direct, transfer, and interlingual machine translation all fall under the realm of RBMT, differing in their depth of source language analysis.

Direct transfer employs a word-by-word translation strategy with basic grammatical adjustments. This process takes place over representations of the source sentence's structure and meaning.

Transfer-based machine translation involves three stages: source text analysis, conversion into target language-oriented representations, and final target text generation.

At the interlingual level, the concept of transfer is substituted by an interlingua. This involves two phases: analyzing the source language text to create an abstract, universal, language-independent representation of meaning, and then generating this meaning using lexical units and syntactic structures of the target language.

Statistical machine translation (SMT) employs statistical models to generate translations from bilingual text corpora. In contrast, example-based machine translation (EBMT) uses parallel bilingual corpora as its primary knowledge source.

Both EBMT and SMT rely on bitext (parallel text pairs) as their foundational data, are empirical in nature, employing machine learning principles rather than being rule-based, and can be enhanced by incorporating more data.

8.24.3 Evaluating machine translation systems

Human evaluators rate translations based on different criteria and provide feedback on specific aspects of the translation. They also compare translations produced by different MT systems or compare MT translations to human reference translations.

NIST uses N-gram precision scores to measure translation quality. It has limitations in capturing all aspects of translation quality.

Error analysis involves identifying and categorizing errors made by machine translation systems to gain insights into their strengths and weaknesses.

User feedback and preference can provide valuable insights into the usability and acceptability of machine translation systems.

A holistic evaluation of MT systems is often used, and evaluation criteria may vary depending on the specific application and use case.

Diverse approaches have been utilized for the evaluation of machine translation. Within the Automatic Language Processing Advisory Committee (ALPAC) report, a study compared various degrees of human translation against machine translation output, employing human participants as evaluators.

Assessing the quality of both human and machine translations involves measuring the informativeness of the translated sentence relative to the original. The study demonstrated a strong correlation between variables, particularly when human judgments were averaged on a per-sentence basis.

The Advanced Research Projects Agency (ARPA) introduced a systematic methodology for evaluating machine translation systems, an approach still in use today. This methodology entailed testing diverse systems grounded in different theoretical frameworks. A selection of methods was then incorporated into subsequent programs.

The quality panel evaluation method was discarded due to logistical complexities and its reliance on a standard US government metric for rating human translations.

In conjunction with a modified comprehension evaluation, monolingual judges rated document segments for adequacy and fluency. This technique effectively covered pertinent aspects of the quality panel evaluation.

BLEU, a metric calculating scores for individual segments and averaging them across the entire corpus, exhibits strong correlation with human quality judgments. It functions as a variation of precision, comparing a candidate translation with multiple reference translations.

Derived from BLEU, the NIST metric gauges the informativeness of specific N-grams. It diverges from BLEU by being less impacted by minor variations in translation length.

METEOR is a novel metric based on the weighted harmonic mean of unigram precision and unigram recall. METEOR introduces unique features like synonym matching and a stemmer, employing modular implementation to facilitate the incorporation of new modules.

A recent addition to MT evaluation metrics, LEPOR combines multiple evaluation factors, including existing ones like precision and recall, along with modified elements such as sentence-length penalty and N-gram-based word order penalty. LEPOR demonstrated higher system-level correlation with human judgments compared to several established metrics.

8.24.4 Case study: Unique features of Indian languages

India is a linguistically diverse country, with hundreds of languages spoken across its regions. Indian languages exhibit several unique characteristics.

Indian languages belong to several language families, including Indo-Aryan, Dravidian, Austroasiatic, Tibeto-Burman, and others.

Indian languages have a rich phonetic inventory with a wide range of consonants and vowels.

Indian languages have diverse writing systems, including Devanagari script, Bengali script, Tamil script, Telugu script, Kannada script, and more.

Many Indian languages exhibit diglossia, where a formal and a colloquial variant coexist. Code-switching is also prevalent in multilingual Indian contexts.

Indian languages have a tendency to form compound words by combining multiple roots or morphemes, and frequently employ agglutination.

Indian languages are diverse and complex, with a multitude of language families, diverse writing systems, phonetic intricacies, rich morphology, and social language norms. Understanding these characteristics is crucial for effective language processing and development of language technologies tailored to the Indian context.

Indian languages have a more sophisticated notion of a character unit called akshara, which consists of 0, 1, 2, or 3 consonants and a vowel. Aksharas can be pronounced independently, and words are made up of one or more aksharas.

There are 10–12 major scripts in India, and each one uses different philosophies for the individual grapheme's and their combinations. The grapheme of one of the consonants is usually at the heart of the printed akshara, and the vowel appears as a matra or vowel modifier.

Indian languages use reduplication in various degrees and for different functions. The next section will introduce echo formations and the final section will review the literature on echo formations in other Dravidian languages.

Onomatopoeic expressions are similar to echo expressions, but have the property that neither of the two halves are independently meaningful. Indian languages display a "predilection for onomatopoeia".

In Hindi, onomatopoeics and expressives are similar, but expressives involve words that are not sound symbolic in the strict sense.

The echo expressions are reduplicated forms that fit between the onomatopoeias and expressives and the paired words and examples of complete and syntactic reduplication. They are highly productive and are a common feature of the Indian subcontinent.

As long as he feeds me, he's called Uncle, but otherwise Kincle. The two halves of the expression are beginning to diverge, and the echo words are said to encode the speaker's affective state.

Information retrieval and lexical resources: Information retrieval is a software program that assists users in finding information from document repositories. It informs the existence and location of documents that might consist of the required information.

A user requests information by formulating a query in natural language, and an information retrieval system responds by retrieving relevant output.

The ad-hoc retrieval problem is a classical problem related to the IR system. It involves entering a query in natural language that describes the required information, and then retrieving the required documents related to the desired information.

The information retrieval model (IR Model) is a mathematical pattern that defines the above-mentioned aspects of retrieval procedure.

The inverted index serves as the central data structure in the majority of information retrieval (IR) systems, facilitating the efficient identification of matches for query words.

Stop words, frequently encountered words with limited search relevance, can be omitted to substantially shrink the size of the inverted index by almost fifty percent.

A query term precisely defines a set of documents. Merging terms using the Boolean AND operator forms a document set that is either equal to or smaller than the document sets of individual terms.

When terms are combined using the Boolean OR operator, the resultant document set is either larger or equal in size to the document sets of any single term.

The vector space model, the simplest framework grounded in sets, solely retrieves exact matches. While its query language is expressive, it can also be intricate.

Beginning this tutorial necessitates a grasp of certain definitions. Tokenization refers to the process of segmenting a string sequence into individual tokens.

Homonyms and stop words, prevalent in language, can pose challenges in linguistic processing.

Before delving into raw text processing, it's essential to understand the architecture of natural language processing (NLP). This involves downloading HTML from a website, tokenizing the text, and normalizing the words.

Initiating with tokenization involves utilizing two functions, namely word_tokenize and sent_tokenize, which accept a string as input and provide a list of tokens as output.

To tokenize your text, you're utilizing the word_tokenize and sent_tokenize functions from the nltk.tokenize module. Employ the strip() function to eliminate occurrences of "n," "t," and spaces from sentences.

8.25 Information Retrieval: Design Aspects of Retrieval Systems

Classical systems use Boolean retrieval, exact matching, and inverted indexes for efficient term-based retrieval.

Non-classical information retrieval systems use probabilistic retrieval models, vector space models, similarity measures, ranked retrieval, partial matching, and fuzzy matching to retrieve information based on a query.

Alternative information retrieval systems use techniques such as semantic analysis, topic modeling, or natural language processing to understand the underlying concepts in documents and queries, provide personalized search results based on user preferences, search history, or user profiles, and retrieve multimedia content across different languages.

Inverted index is the primary data structure of most IR systems. It makes it easy to search for hits of a query word.

Stop words are commonly occurring words that are considered to have limited utility in search contexts. These words are compiled into a list known as a stop list, and their inclusion can substantially decrease the size of the inverted index.

We can explain the Boolean AND operator by saying that it returns a document set that is smaller than or equal to the set of documents that are indexed with any of the single terms.

Upon employing the Boolean OR operator to merge terms, the resultant document set surpasses in size or remains equal to the document sets generated by any of the individual terms.

8.26 Exploring Information Retrieval Models: Classical, Non-classical, Alternativ

The vector space model signifies documents and queries as vectors in a high-dimensional space, and ranks documents based on their similarity to queries.

Latent semantic indexing (LSI) uses singular value decomposition (SVD) to identify latent semantic relationships between terms and documents.

Latent Dirichlet allocation (LDA) is a topic modeling technique that can be used to retrieve documents associated with a query.

Neural network models have been applied to information retrieval to improve the accuracy and effectiveness of retrieval systems.

Reinforcement learning-based models use techniques from reinforcement learning to optimize information retrieval, and combine multiple models or incorporate elements from various models.

8.27 Understanding Lexical Resources

Lexical resources are used in information retrieval to enhance the effectiveness and accuracy of retrieval systems.

WordNet is a lexical resource that organizes words into synsets and provides semantic relationships between them.

Lexical normalization models use stemming, lemmatization, or morphological analysis to normalize terms and retrieve documents that match the underlying concept.

Lexical disambiguation uses resources like WordNet and sense inventories to resolve word sense ambiguity. This enhances the accuracy of retrieval.

Named entity recognition (NER) models identify and categorize named entities in text documents. Lexical resources contribute to information retrieval by expanding queries, capturing semantic relationships, normalizing and disambiguating terms, and leveraging domain-specific knowledge.

8.27.1 Word Embeddings

Word embeddings are a technique used in natural language processing and information retrieval to represent words as numerical vectors.

Word embeddings are high-dimensional vectors that represent different aspects of a word.

Training word embeddings involves presenting words to a neural network, which adjusts the word vectors based on the context.

Word embeddings allow for measuring the similarity and distance between words based on the geometric properties of the vector space.

Word embeddings can capture various linguistic relationships and analogies, such as "king – man + woman".

Pretrained word embeddings can be used for various NLP tasks, even when the specific domain or dataset is different from the original training data.

8.27.2 Word2Vec

Word2Vec is a popular algorithm for learning word embeddings that captures the semantic and syntactic relationships between words.

Word2Vec employs two main training methods: Continuous bag of words (CBOW) and Skip-gram. CBOW is faster to train and works well for frequently occurring words, while Skip-gram is slower but performs better for infrequent or rare words.

Word2Vec employs negative sampling to improve training efficiency and lead to more meaningful word representations.

Word2Vec embeddings enable measuring the similarity between words using cosine similarity, and also allow for finding analogies by performing vector operations.

8.27.3 GloVe

GloVe embeddings are used in natural language processing tasks such as word similarity, text classification, machine translation, and information retrieval. They can be used as initializations or directly integrated into NLP models.

In this study, our focus is on analyzing how lemmatization and part-of-speech disambiguation impact the performance of word embeddings. We explore their effects within a unique evaluation framework based on resources, as well as through the lens of established similarity benchmarks. Our findings reveal that these two techniques yield complementary qualitative outcomes and influence the vocabulary composition. We conclude that the optimal approach involves utilizing both strategies together to achieve the best results.

Word2Vec is a technique used for learning word association in a natural language processing task. It uses a neural network model and uses a list of numbers to represent any distinct word.

The continuous bag of words (CBOW) method and the Skip-gram method are used to predict the words that can be fitted into the middle of a partial incomplete sentence based on the surrounding context of the words.

GloVe is a model used for the representation of the distributed words. It uses an unsupervised learning algorithm and is developed as an open-source project at Stanford.

The GloVe model uses the matrix factorization technique for word embedding on the word-context matrix.

By considering the unique words from two sentences, we can compute the ratio of probabilities between any two pairs of words, and by this we can infer that "fast" is more relevant than "the".

Word2vec is a predictive model that uses trainable embedding weights to predict context words.

The GloVe technique factors the word-context matrix to make it a lower-dimensional matrix, where each row is a vector representation for each word.

The GloVe method uses a loss function to make a lower-dimensional matrix, and a better word embedding can be obtained by making the reconstruction loss lower.

Word2vec employs a three-layer neural network that uses the co-occurrence matrix for learning the linear relationship between words.

The word2vec produced word embedding can hold the word vectors such as "king" - "man" + "woman" -> "queen" together or close in the vector space, where GloVe cannot understand such linear relationships.

Word2Vec employs negative sampling and converts the softmax function as the sigmoid function, making it faster in the computation than GloVe.

We discussed Word2Vec and GloVe models, saw how gensim provides an API for using these models, and associated both models based on various important parameters.

8.27.4 Unsupervised methods in NLP

Matrix factorization is another technique for unsupervised NLP machine learning. It uses latent factors to break a large matrix down into two smaller matrices.

Topic modeling algorithms aim to uncover latent topics in a collection of documents by analyzing the co-occurrence patterns of words.

Word embeddings signify words as dense vector representations in a continuous space, and are used for downstream NLP tasks.

Unsupervised anomaly detection methods can be used to detect unusual or outlier instances in a dataset.

Unsupervised learning techniques can be used to create dense vector representations of entire sentences or paragraphs, facilitating tasks such as sentence similarity, sentiment analysis, and text classification.

8.28 Harnessing Graphical Models for Sequence Labeling

Hidden Markov models and conditional random fields are powerful tools for sequence labeling in natural language processing.

HMMs are generative models that assume a hidden state sequence generates an observed sequence. They are often used for tasks like part-of-speech tagging.

Hidden Markov models are probabilistic graphical models widely used for sequential data modeling, including sequence labeling tasks in natural language processing.

During training, the parameters of the HMM are estimated using maximum likelihood estimation or other statistical estimation techniques.

HMMs have been widely used for various NLP tasks, but the Markov property assumption might not always hold in complex NLP scenarios.

Conditional random fields (CRFs) are discriminative models that model the conditional probability of a sequence given the observed features. They are widely used in NLP for tasks such as named entity recognition, chunking, and semantic role labeling.

HMMs and CRFs both have their strengths and weaknesses, and the choice between the two be contingent on the specific task and the characteristics of the data.

Conditional random fields are probabilistic graphical models that are commonly used for sequence labeling tasks in natural language processing (NLP). CRFs extend hidden Markov models by relaxing the "Markov assumption" that the current state only depends on the previous state.

During training, CRFs use techniques like maximum likelihood estimation to find the limits that maximize the conditional likelihood of the true labels given the observed sequence. During inference, CRFs use techniques like belief propagation.

9

Conclusion

NLP or natural language processing has soul searched itself to make computers talk, comprehend and create human languages in a way it has impacted various domains. NLP for example through methods like sentiment analysis, language translation, and text summarization has greatly improved how people interface technologies. Recent procedures like text preprocessing, syntactic analysis, and semantic analysis, which are described in this book, are part of NLP that is applied to more advanced forms of the procedures. And whereas previous research depended on statistical models, rule systems, in the newest developments of NLP with deep learning, particularly with the help of transformers, new walls have been broken driving the technology to new heights of accuracy in language processing.

As for the future perspectives, NLP has a great prospect in addressing the present problems and developing new applications. It safely assumed that advancement in multilingual models, context handling, and low-resource language support will further extend the applicability of NLP. However, problems such as vagueness of language, how to deal with idioms, and ethical issues still present research issues of concern. As NLP technology progresses, the incorporation into industries like healthcare, customer service and education will not only change industries but also change the way people interact with the technology to make it more easily used by everyone.

References

[1]   Manning, C. D., & Schütze, H. (1999). **Foundations of Statistical Natural Language Processing**. MIT Press.

[2]   Jurafsky, D., & Martin, J. H. (2020). **Speech and Language Processing**. Pearson.

[3]   Bird, S., Klein, E., & Loper, E. (2009). **Natural Language Processing with Python**. O'Reilly Media.

[4]   Vaswani, A., et al. (2017). **Attention Is All You Need**. Advances in Neural Information Processing Systems.

[5]   Devlin, J., et al. (2019). **BERT: Pre-training of Deep Bidirectional Transformers for Language Understanding**. NAACL-HLT.

[6]   Mikolov, T., et al. (2013). **Efficient Estimation of Word Representations in Vector Space**. arXiv preprint arXiv:1301.3781.

[7]   Pennington, J., Socher, R., & Manning, C. (2014). **GloVe: Global Vectors for Word Representation**. EMNLP.

[8]   Peters, M. E., et al. (2018). **Deep Contextualized Word Representations**. NAACL-HLT.

[9]   Goldberg, Y. (2017). **Neural Network Methods for Natural Language Processing**. Morgan & Claypool Publishers.

[10] LeCun, Y., Bengio, Y., & Hinton, G. (2015). **Deep Learning**. Nature.

[11] Sutskever, I., Vinyals, O., & Le, Q. V. (2014). **Sequence to Sequence Learning with Neural Networks**. Advances in Neural Information Processing Systems.

[12] Bahdanau, D., Cho, K., & Bengio, Y. (2015). **Neural Machine Translation by Jointly Learning to Align and Translate**. ICLR.

[13] Young, T., et al. (2018). **Recent Trends in Deep Learning Based Natural Language Processing**. IEEE Computational Intelligence Magazine.

[14] Liu, Y., et al. (2019). **RoBERTa: A Robustly Optimized BERT Pretraining Approach**. arXiv preprint arXiv:1907.11692.

[15]   Ruder, S., et al. (2019). **Transfer Learning in Natural Language Processing**. Journal of Artificial Intelligence Research.

[16]   Sennrich, R., Haddow, B., & Birch, A. (2016). **Neural Machine Translation of Rare Words with Subword Units**. ACL.

[17]   Vaswani, A., et al. (2013). **Transformer: Attention is All You Need**. Advances in Neural Information Processing Systems.

[18]   Howard, J., & Ruder, S. (2018). **Universal Language Model Fine-tuning for Text Classification**. ACL.

[19]   Cho, K., et al. (2014). **Learning Phrase Representations Using RNN Encoder-Decoder for Statistical Machine Translation**. EMNLP.

[20]   Radford, A., et al. (2019). **Language Models are Unsupervised Multitask Learners**. OpenAI Blog.

[21]   Brown, T. B., et al. (2020). **Language Models are Few-Shot Learners**. NeurIPS.

[22]   Cambria, E., et al. (2020). **SenticNet 6: Ensemble Application of Symbolic and Subsymbolic AI for Sentiment Analysis**. CIKM.

[23]   Zhang, Y., & Yang, Q. (2017). **A Survey on Multi-task Learning**. IEEE Transactions on Knowledge and Data Engineering.

[24]   Hinton, G., et al. (2012). **Deep Neural Networks for Acoustic Modeling in Speech Recognition: The Shared Views of Four Research Groups**. IEEE Signal Processing Magazine.

[25]   Bengio, Y., et al. (2003). **A Neural Probabilistic Language Model**. Journal of Machine Learning Research.

[26]   Li, J., et al. (2020). **XLM-R: A Large-Scale Pretrained Cross-Lingual Language Model**. EMNLP.

[27]   Socher, R., et al. (2013). **Recursive Deep Models for Semantic Compositionality Over a Sentiment Treebank**. EMNLP.

[28]   Graves, A., Mohamed, A.-r., & Hinton, G. (2013). **Speech Recognition with Deep Recurrent Neural Networks**. IEEE International Conference on Acoustics, Speech, and Signal Processing.

[29]   Dos Santos, C. N., & Gatti, M. (2014). **Deep Convolutional Neural Networks for Sentiment Analysis of Short Texts**. COLING.

[30]   Collobert, R., et al. (2011). **Natural Language Processing (almost) from Scratch**. Journal of Machine Learning Research.

Index

D

deep learning NLP 2

L

language modeling 11, 27, 49, 52, 53, 54, 55, 117, 127, 129

M

machine translation 2, 3, 4, 11, 33, 38, 41, 51, 73, 80, 81, 84, 106, 128, 135, 137, 138, 140

N

Natural language processing (NLP) 1, 2, 4, 17, 20, 32, 57, 62, 75, 80, 99, 111, 120, 130, 145, 149

named entity recognition (NER) 4, 9, 12, 21, 26, 58, 103, 115, 117, 145

S

sentiment analysis 1, 3, 14, 21, 22, 58, 104, 117, 126, 149

T

text preprocessing 1, 21, 28, 124, 149

For Product Safety Concerns and Information please contact our EU
representative GPSR@taylorandfrancis.com
Taylor & Francis Verlag GmbH, Kaufingerstraße 24, 80331 München, Germany

www.ingramcontent.com/pod-product-compliance
Lightning Source LLC
Chambersburg PA
CBHW070727220326
41598CB00024BA/3330

9 788877 004829 3